Unfortunately, It Was Paradise

Mahmoud Darwish

Unfortunately, It Was Paradise

Selected Poems

Translated and Edited by
Munir Akash and Carolyn Forché
(with Sinan Antoon and Amira El-Zein)

University of California Press   Berkeley · Los Angeles · London

University of California Press
Berkeley and Los Angeles, California

University of California Press, Ltd.
London, England

Library of Congress Cataloging-in-Publication Data

Darwish, Mahmoud.
    [Poems. English. Selections]
    Unfortunately, it was paradise : selected poems / Mahmoud Darwish ; translated and
    edited by Munir Akash and Carolyn Forché, with Sinan Antoon and Amira El-Zein.
        p. cm.
    ISBN 0-520-23753-6 (cloth : alk. paper)—ISBN 0-520-23754-4 (paper : alk. paper)
    I. Akash, Munir.   II. Forché, Carolyn.   III. Title.

PJ7820.A7 A22   2003
892'.716—dc21   2002068454

Manufactured in Canada

10 09 08 07 06 05 04 03
10 9 8 7 6 5 4 3 2 1

The paper used in this publication meets the minimum requirements
of ANSI/NISO Z39.48-1992 (R 1997) (*Permanence of Paper*). ∞

The publisher gratefully acknowledges
the generous contribution to this book
provided by the Lannan Foundation.

Pero yo ya no soy yo
Ni mi casa es ya mi casa.

But now I am no longer I,
nor is my house any longer my house.

Federico García Lorca

Contents

x

from A Bed for the Stranger (1999)

Mural *(2000)*

Three Poems *(before 1986)*

Acknowledgments

Any collection of this sort requires the support and assistance of more people than can be named here. Each of them knows who he or she is, and to each of them many thanks. I offer my sincere appreciation to the Lannan Foundation for their generosity and their unfailing support. Patrick Lannan and the wonderful family of his foundation by their insight, bravery, and service to humanity have taught me dedication. Special thanks to the poet Mahmoud Darwish for his patience in answering my many questions and, of course, for his guidance and very helpful comments along the way. Each poem in this collection has been carefully selected from Darwish's entire work in collaboration with the poet himself.

This enterprise could not have been possible without an exceptional team of translators. All have known Darwish and his work for a long time. When I expressed to Mahmoud Darwish my desire to translate this collection, he asked me to work in collaboration with a leading American poet who could give the translations a single consistent tone. What Carolyn Forché has done here, in this very short period of time, is an enterprise short of miraculous. She recreated the poems translated with a different sensibility and made them harmonious in a single voice. For this and for her wholehearted dedication I can't thank her enough. A heartfelt expression of gratitude to Daniel Moore and Laura Cerruti for their painstaking review and exceptional editorial expertise. Their drive, vision, and unique poetic sensibility turned a dream into reality.

Very special thanks to Harry Mattison, Ibrahim Muhawi, and Kinda Akash for their insightful reading and their many helpful suggestions, and to Caroline Roberts and Kaia Sand for their meticulous copy editing. Grateful acknowledgment is made to the editors and publishers of the following journals in which some of these poems were first published: *Tikkun, Salmagundi, Brick, American Poetry Review,* and *Fence.*

Finally, I have to admit that all the great work in this collection exists thanks to these wonderful people and that every mistake in it is mine.

Munir Akash

Introduction

Mahmoud Darwish is a literary rarity. Critically acclaimed as one of the most important poets in the Arabic language and beloved as the voice of his people, he is an artist demanding of his work continual transformation and a living legend whose lyrics are sung by fieldworkers and schoolchildren. Few poets have borne such disparately bestowed adulation, nor survived such dramatic vicissitudes of history and fate as Mahmoud Darwish; even fewer have done so while endeavoring to open new possibilities for poetry while assimilating one of the world's oldest literary traditions. His poetry has been enthusiastically embraced since the publication of his first volume, *Leaves of Olive,* in 1964. After the Arab defeat in the 1967 war, Darwish raised his voice in searing lyrics confronting the pain of everyday life for Palestinians. In a realism stripped of poetic flourish, the "poetry of resistance" was born. With Nerudian transparency, his poems of the sixties and early seventies reflected his pain over the occupation of his homeland and his lingering hopes for its liberation. In the intervening years, the poetry of Darwish exemplified a brilliant artistic restlessness, with each volume opening new formal territory and poetic concerns. With the publication of this collection, Darwish will celebrate his sixty-first birthday and nearly four decades of writing. He is the poet laureate of Palestine—a poet sharing the fate of his people, living in a town under siege, while providing them with a language for their anguish and dreams. Any serious study of his work must take into account the context in which it was written:

the years of exilic wandering and survival; the aesthetic, metaphysical, and po-
litical struggles particular to this poet.

Mahmoud Darwish was born in the village of Birwe, in the district of Akka
(Acre) in upper Galilee, Palestine, on March 13, 1942. When he was six years
old, the Israeli Army occupied and subsequently destroyed Birwe, along with
416 other Palestinian villages. To avoid the ensuing massacres, the Darwish
family fled to Lebanon. A year later, they returned to their country "illegally,"
and settled in the nearby village of Dayr al-Asad, but too late to be counted
among the Palestinians who survived and remained within the borders of the
new state. The young Darwish was now an "internal refugee," legally classified
as a "present-absent alien," a species of Orwellian doublethink that the poet
would later interrogate in his lyric meditation "The Owl's Night," wherein the
present is "placeless, transient, absurd," and absence "mysterious," "human,"
and "unwanted," "going about its own preoccupations and piling up its chosen
objects. Like a small jar of water," he writes, "absence breaks in me." The newly
"alienated" Palestinians fell under military rule and were sent into a complex
legal maze of emergency rulings. They could not travel within their homeland
without permission, nor, apparently, could the eight-year-old Darwish recite a
poem of lamentation at the school celebration of the second anniversary of Is-
rael without subsequently incurring the wrath of the Israeli military governor.
Thereafter he was obliged to hide whenever an Israeli officer appeared. Dur-
ing his school years, and until he left the country in 1970, Darwish would be
imprisoned several times and frequently harassed, always for the crimes of re-
citing his poetry and traveling without a permit from village to village.

Birwe was erased from land and map, but remained intact in memory, the
mirage of a lost paradise. In 1997, the Israeli-French filmmaker, Simone Bit-
ton, went to what had been Birwe to film Darwish's childhood landscape, but
found nothing but ruins and a desolate, weed-choked cemetery. On April 16,
2001, Israeli bulldozers began paving a new road through the graves, unearth-
ing human remains throughout the site. The vanished Palestinian village be-
came, for the displaced poet, a bundle of belongings carried on the back of the

refugee. Denied the recognition of citizenship in the new state, Darwish settled on language as his identity, and took upon himself the task of restoration of meaning and thus, homeland:

> Who am I? This is a question that others ask, but has no answer.
> I am my language, I am an ode, two odes, ten. This is my language.
> I am my language . . .   ("A Rhyme for the Odes," 91)

> We travel like everyone else, but we return to nothing . . .
> Ours is a country of words: Talk. Talk.   ("We Travel Like All People," 11)

In 1996, after twenty-six years of exile, Darwish was granted a permit to visit his family and was warmly embraced by his compatriots, the "internal refugees." Thousands of cheering Palestinians greeted him in a festive way, chanting his popular poems. Darwish later reflected on the pain and longing he felt for his homeland: "As long as my soul is alive no one can smother my feeling of nostalgia for my country which I still consider as Palestine."

Darwish's twentieth book of poems, the recently published *Mural,* fuses lyric and epic in an impassioned meditation on the whole of his life and his own confrontation with mortality. The realized ambitions of this poem exemplify the poet's impressive range. Assimilating centuries of Arabic poetic forms and applying the chisel of modern sensibility to the richly veined ore of its literary past, Darwish subjected his art to the impress of exile and to his own demand that the work remain true to itself, independent of its critical or public reception. He has, as an artist, repeatedly confounded expectations, without shirking the role assigned to him by his peoples' historical experience. Perhaps no poet in our time has borne this weight: to be the esteemed and revered voice of a people, while remaining true to poetry itself, however hermetic and interior—to be at once culturally multiple and spiritually singular. His poetry is both the linguistic fruit of an internalized collective memory and an impassioned poetic response to his long absorption of regional and international poetic movements. As much as he is the voice of the Palestinian diaspora, he is the voice of the fragmented soul.

It is the soul of Palestine that Darwish has made resonant in his work, giving it presence in the midst of suffering and hardship. Moving from city to city, exile to exile, he has written out of a distinctly Palestinian sensibility and conscience, out of the richness of Palestine's cultural past and a belief in its common destiny. At the same time, he has become a poet and citizen of the world.

Darwish's poetic fraternity includes Federico García Lorca's *canto hondo* (deep song), Pablo Neruda's bardic epic range, Osip Mandelstam's elegiac poignancy, and Yehuda Amichai's sensitive lyric responsiveness to the contemporary history of the region. As a poet of exilic being, he resembles C. P. Cavafy, and shares with other poet-exiles of the past century a certain understanding of the exilic condition of literary art. Although his later collections became more universal in outlook, they are also a powerful outcry and statement of anguish—both of the topography of the soul and the calamity of his people. They lament the degeneration of the human condition and strive to stimulate latent forces to create a new destiny. If any particular obsession is sustained throughout his oeuvre, it would be the question of subjectivity itself, not only the mutability of identity, but its otherness. It is the spiritual dimension of what was, unfortunately, paradise, that he has most sustained in his life and work.

"I have found that the land is fragile," he said in *Palestine As Metaphor:*

and the sea, light; I have learned that language and metaphor are not enough to restore place to a place. . . . Not having been able to find my place on earth, I have attempted to find it in History, and History cannot be reduced to a compensation for lost geography. It is also a vantage point for shadows, for the self and the Other, apprehended in a more complex human journey. . . . Is this a simple, artistic ruse, a simple borrowing? Or is it despair taking shape? The answer has no importance. The essential thing for me is that I have found a greater lyrical capacity, a passage from the relative to the absolute, an opening for me to inscribe the national within the universal, for Palestine not to be limited to Palestine, but to establish its aesthetic legitimacy in a greater human sphere.[1]

It is our hope that this volume, and the recently published collection, *The Adam of Two Edens*,[2] will extend his readership in the English-speaking world in this time of calamity in the poet's homeland.

Munir Akash
Carolyn Forché
Bethesda, Maryland
August 2001

1. Mahmoud Darwish, *La Palestine comme métaphore Entretiens* (Paris: Sindhad, Actes Sud, 1997), 25.

2. Mahmoud Darwish, *The Adam of Two Edens,* ed. and with introduction by Munir Akash (Syracuse: Syracuse University Press, 2000).

from

Fewer Roses

1986

Translated by Munir Akash and Carolyn Forché

I Will Slog over This Road

I will slog over this endless road to its end.
Until my heart stops, I will slog over this endless, endless road
with nothing to lose but the dust, what has died in me, and a row of palms
pointing toward what vanishes. I will pass the row of palms.
The wound does not need its poet to paint the blood of death like a pomegranate!
On the roof of neighing, I will cut thirty openings for meaning
so that you may end one trail only so as to begin another.
Whether this earth comes to an end or not, we'll slog over this endless road.
More tense than a bow. Our steps, be arrows. Where were we a moment ago?
Shall we join, in a while, the first arrow? The spinning wind whirled us.
So, what do you say?

I say: *I will slog over this endless road to its end and my own.*

Another Road in the Road

There is yet another road in the road, another chance for migration.

To cross over we will throw many roses in the river.

No widow wants to return to us, there we have to go, north of the
neighing horses.

Have yet we forgotten something, both simple and worthy of our new ideas?

When you talk about yesterday, friend, I see my face reflected in the song
of doves.

I touch the dove's ring and hear flute-song in the abandoned fig tree.

My longing weeps for everything. My longing shoots back at me, to kill or
be killed.

Yet there is another road in the road, and on and on. So where are the
questions taking me?

I am from here, I am from there, yet am neither here nor there.

I will have to throw many roses before I reach a rose in Galilee.

Were It Up to Me to Begin Again

Were it up to me to begin again, I would make the same choice. Roses on
  the fence.
I would travel the same roads that might or might not lead to Cordoba.
I would lay my shadow down on two rocks, so that birds could nest on one of
  the boughs.
I would break open my shadow for the scent of almond to float in a cloud of dust
and grow tired on the slopes. Come closer, and listen.
Share my bread, drink my wine, don't leave me alone like a tired willow.
I love lands not trod over by songs of migration, or become subject to
  passions of blood and desire.
I love women whose hidden desires make horses put an end to their lives at
  the threshold.
If I return, I will return to the same rose and follow the same steps.
But never to Cordoba.

On This Earth

We have on this earth what makes life worth living: April's hesitation, the
    aroma of bread
at dawn, a woman's point of view about men, the works of Aeschylus, the
    beginning
of love, grass on a stone, mothers living on a flute's sigh and the invaders' fear
    of memories.

We have on this earth what makes life worth living: the final days of
    September, a woman
keeping her apricots ripe after forty, the hour of sunlight in prison, a cloud
    reflecting a swarm
of creatures, the peoples' applause for those who face death with a smile,
a tyrant's fear of songs.

We have on this earth what makes life worth living: on this earth, the Lady
    of Earth,
mother of all beginnings and ends. She was called Palestine. Her name
    later became
Palestine. My Lady, because you are my Lady, I deserve life.

I Belong There

I belong there. I have many memories. I was born as everyone is born.

I have a mother, a house with many windows, brothers, friends, and a prison cell with a chilly window! I have a wave snatched by seagulls, a panorama of my own. I have a saturated meadow. In the deep horizon of my word, I have a moon, a bird's sustenance, and an immortal olive tree.

I have lived on the land long before swords turned man into prey.

I belong there. When heaven mourns for her mother, I return heaven to
   her mother.

And I cry so that a returning cloud might carry my tears.

To break the rules, I have learned all the words needed for a trial by blood.

I have learned and dismantled all the words in order to draw from them a
   single word: *Home.*

Addresses for the Soul, outside This Place

I love to travel . . .
to a village that never hangs my last evening on its cypresses. I love the trees
that witnessed how two birds suffered at our hands, how we raised the stones.
Wouldn't it be better if we raised our days
to grow slowly and embrace this greenness? I love the rainfall
on the women of distant meadows. I love the glittering water and the scent
   of stone.
Wouldn't it be better if we defied our ages
and gazed much longer at the last sky before moonset?
Addresses for the soul, outside this place. I love to travel
to any wind . . . But I don't love to arrive.

Earth Presses against Us

Earth is pressing against us, trapping us in the final passage.

To pass through, we pull off our limbs.

Earth is squeezing us. If only we were its wheat, we might die and yet live.

If only it were our mother so that she might temper us with mercy.

If only we were pictures of rocks held in our dreams like mirrors.

We glimpse faces in their final battle for the soul, of those who will be killed

by the last living among us. We mourn their children's feast.

We saw the faces of those who would throw our children out of the windows

of this last space. A star to burnish our mirrors.

Where should we go after the last border? Where should birds fly after the

    last sky?

Where should plants sleep after the last breath of air?

We write our names with crimson mist!

We end the hymn with our flesh.

Here we will die. Here, in the final passage.

Here or there, our blood will plant olive trees.

We Journey towards a Home

We journey towards a home not of our flesh. Its chestnut trees are not of
  our bones.
Its rocks are not like goats in the mountain hymn. The pebbles' eyes are
  not lilies.
We journey towards a home that does not halo our heads with a special sun.
Mythical women applaud us. A sea for us, a sea against us.
When water and wheat are not at hand, eat our love and drink our tears . . .
There are mourning scarves for poets. A row of marble statues will lift our voice.
And an urn to keep the dust of time away from our souls. Roses for us and
  against us.
You have your glory, we have ours. Of our home we see only the unseen:
  our mystery.
Glory is ours: a throne carried on feet torn by roads that led to every home
  but our own!
The soul must recognize itself in its very soul, or die here.

We Travel Like All People

We travel like everyone else, but we return to nothing. As if travel were
a path of clouds. We buried our loved ones in the shade of clouds and
  between roots of trees.
We said to our wives: *Give birth for hundreds of years, so that we may end
  this journey*
within an hour of a country, within a meter of the impossible!
We travel in the chariots of the Psalms, sleep in the tents of the prophets,
  and are born again in the language of Gypsies.
We measure space with a hoopoe's beak, and sing so that distance may forget us.
We cleanse the moonlight. Your road is long, so dream of seven women to bear
this long journey on your shoulders. Shake the trunks of palm trees for them.
You know the names, and which one will give birth to the Son of Galilee.
Ours is a country of words: Talk. Talk. Let me rest my road against a stone.
Ours is a country of words: Talk. Talk. Let me see an end to this journey.

Athens Airport

Athens airport disperses us to other airports. *Where can I fight?* asks the fighter.

Where can I deliver your child? a pregnant woman shouts back.

Where can I invest my money? asks the officer.

This is none of my business, the intellectual says.

Where did you come from? asks the customs' official.

And we answer: *From the sea!*

Where are you going?

To the sea, we answer.

What is your address?

A woman of our group says: *My village is the bundle on my back.*

We have waited in the Athens airport for years.

A young man marries a girl but they have no place for their wedding night.

He asks: *Where can I make love to her?*

We laugh and say: *This is not the right time for that question.*

The analyst says: *In order to live, they die by mistake.*

The literary man says: *Our camp will certainly fall.*

What do they want from us?

Athens airport welcomes its visitors without end.

Yet, like the benches in the terminal, we remain, impatiently waiting for
the sea.

How many more years longer, O Athens airport?

I Talk Too Much

I talk too much about the slightest nuance between women and trees,
about the earth's enchantment, about a country with no passport stamp.
I ask: *Is it true, good ladies and gentlemen, that the earth of Man is for all
human beings*
as you say? In that case, where is my little cottage, and where am I?
The conference audiences applaud me for another three minutes,
three minutes of freedom and recognition.
The conference approves our right of return,
like all chickens and horses, to a dream made of stone.
I shake hands with them, one by one. I bow to them. Then I continue my journey
to another country and talk about the difference between a mirage and the rain.
I ask: *Is it true, good ladies and gentlemen, that the earth of Man is for all
human beings?*

We Have the Right to Love Autumn

And we, too, have the right to love the last days of autumn and ask:
Is there room in the field for a new autumn, so we may lie down like coals?
An autumn that blights its leaves with gold.
If only we were leaves on a fig tree, or even neglected meadow plants
that we may observe the seasons change!
If only we never said goodbye to the fundamentals
and questioned our fathers when they fled at knife point. May poetry and
    God's name have mercy on us!
We have the right to warm the nights of beautiful women, and talk about
what might shorten the night of two strangers waiting for the North to reach
    the compass.
It's autumn. We have the right to smell autumn's fragrances and ask the night
    for a dream.
Does the dream, like the dreamers themselves, sicken? *Autumn. Autumn.*
Can a people be born on a guillotine?
We have the right to die any way we wish.
May the earth hide itself away in an ear of wheat!

The Last Train Has Stopped

The last train has stopped at the last platform. No one is there
to save the roses, no doves to alight on a woman made of words.
Time has ended. The ode fares no better than the foam.
Don't put faith in our trains, love. Don't wait for anyone in the crowd.
The last train has stopped at the last platform. But no one
can cast the reflection of Narcissus back on the mirrors of night.
Where can I write my latest account of the body's incarnation?
It's the end of what was bound to end! Where is that which ends?
Where can I free myself of the homeland in my body?
Don't put faith in our trains, love. The last dove flew away.
The last train has stopped at the last platform. And no one was there.

On the Slope, Higher Than the Sea, They Slept

On the slope, higher than the sea, higher than the cypresses, they slept.
The iron sky erased their memories, and the dove flew away
in the direction of their pointing fingers, east of their torn bodies.
Weren't they entitled to throw the basil of their names on the moon in the water?
And plant bitter orange trees in the ditches to dispel the darkness?

They sleep beyond the limits of space, on a slope where words turn to stone.
They sleep on a stone carved from the bones of their phoenix.
Our heart can celebrate their feast in nearly no time.
Our heart can steal a place for doves to return to earth's bedrock.
O kin sleeping within me, at the ends of the earth: peace be unto you! Peace.

He Embraces His Murderer

He embraces his murderer. May he win his heart: Do you feel angrier if
    I survive?
Brother . . . My brother! What did I do to make you destroy me?
Two birds fly overhead. Why don't you shoot upward? What do you say?
You grew tired of my embrace and my smell. Aren't you just as tired of the
    fear within me?
Then throw your gun in the river! What do you say?
The enemy on the riverbank aims his machine gun at an embrace? Shoot
    the enemy!
Thus we avoid the enemy's bullets and keep from falling into sin.
What do you say? You'll kill me so the enemy can go home to our home
and descend again into the law of the jungle?
What did you do with my mother's coffee, with *your* mother's coffee?
What crime did I commit to make you destroy me?
I will never cease embracing you.

And I will never release you.

Winds Shift against Us

Winds shift against us. The southern wind blows with our enemies.

   The passage narrows.

We flash victory signs in the darkness, so the darkness may glitter.

We fly as if riding the trees of a dream. O ends of the earth! O difficult
   dream! Will you go on?

For the thousandth time we write on the last breath of air. We die so they do
   not prevail!

We run after the echo of our voices. May we find a moon there.

We sing for the rocks. May the rocks be startled.

We engrave our bodies with iron for a river to billow up.

Winds shift against us. North wind with southern wind, and we shout:

   Where can we settle?

We ask mythical women for relatives who would rather see us dead.

An eagle settles on our bodies, and we chase after dreams. May we find them.

They soar behind us to find us here. There is no escape!

We live our death. This half-death is our triumph.

Neighing on the Slope

Horses' neighing on the slope. Downward or upward.
I prepare my portrait for my woman to hang on a wall when I die.
She says: *Is there a wall to hang it on?*
I say: *We'll build a room for it. Where? In any house.*

Horses' neighing on the slope. Downward or upward.

Does a woman in her thirties need a homeland to put a picture in a frame?
Can I reach the summit of this rugged mountain? The slope is either an
    abyss or a place of siege.
Midway it divides. What a journey! Martyrs killing one another.
I prepare my portrait for my woman. When a new horse neighs in you, tear it up.

Horses' neighing on the slope. Upward, or upward.

Other Barbarians Will Come

Other barbarians will come. The emperor's wife will be abducted. Drums will beat loudly. Drums will beat so that horses will leap over human bodies from the Aegean Sea to the Dardanelles. So why should we be concerned? What do our wives have to do with horse racing?

The emperor's wife will be abducted. Drums will beat loudly and other barbarians will come. Barbarians will fill the cities' emptiness, slightly higher than the sea, mightier than the sword in a time of madness. So why should we be concerned? What do our children have to do with the children of this impudence?

Drums will beat loudly and other barbarians will come. The emperor's wife will be taken from his bedroom. From his bedroom he will launch a military assault to return his bedmate to his bed. Why should we be concerned? What do fifty thousand victims have to do with this brief marriage?

Can Homer be born after us . . . and myths open their doors to the throng?

They Would Love to See Me Dead

They would love to see me dead, to say: *He belongs to us, he is ours.*

For twenty years I have heard their footsteps on the walls of the night.

They open no door, yet here they are now. I see three of them:

a poet, a killer, and a reader of books.

Will you have some wine? I asked.

Yes, they answered.

When do you plan to shoot me? I asked.

Take it easy, they answered.

They lined up their glasses all in a row and started singing for the people.

I asked: *When will you begin my assassination?*

Already done, they said . . . *Why did you send your shoes on ahead to your soul?*

So it can wander the face of the earth, I said.

The earth is wickedly dark, so why is your poem so white?

Because my heart is teeming with thirty seas, I answered.

They asked: *Why do you love French wine?*

Because I ought to love the most beautiful women, I answered.

They asked: *How would you like your death?*

Blue, like stars pouring from a window—would you like more wine?

Yes, we'll drink, they said.

Please take your time. I want you to kill me slowly so I can write my last

poem to my heart's wife. They laughed, and took from me

only the words dedicated to my heart's wife.

When the Martyrs Go to Sleep

When the martyrs go to sleep, I wake to protect them from professional
mourners.

I say: *Have a good morning at home, a home of clouds and trees, a mirage
of water.*

I congratulate them on their safety from injury, and the generosity of
the slaughterhouse.

I take time so they can take me from time. Are we all martyrs?

I whisper: *Friends, at least save us one wall for our laundry lines, and one
night for songs.*

I hang your names wherever you wish, so go to sleep. Sleep on the trellis of
that sour vine.

I protect your dreams from your guards' knives, from the revolt
of the scriptures themselves against the prophets.

When you go to sleep tonight, be a song for those who have no songs.

I say: *Have a good morning, a home carried on the back of a wild horse.*

Then I whisper: *Friends, never be like us, a gallows in disguise.*

The Night There

The night there is pitch black . . . and roses are fewer.
The road will fork even more than before. The valley will split open
and the slope will collapse on us. The wound opens wide. Relatives flee.
Victims kill each other to erase their victims' sight and find relief.
We'll know more than we knew before. One abyss will lead to another.
When we embrace an idea worshipped by tribes and branded on their
    vanishing bodies,
we'll witness emperors engraving their names on grains of wheat to show
    their power.
Aren't we changed? Men follow the teachings of the sword
and spill blood. Let the sand pile up.
Women who believe in what's between their thighs follow the teachings of
    lewdness.
Let the shadow shrink.

Yet, I will follow the path of the song, even though my roses are fewer.

We Went to Aden

We went to Aden ahead of our dreams. The moon was shining
on the wing of a crow. We gazed at the sea.
For whom does the sea toll these bells? To let us hear our own rhythms?

We went to Aden in advance of our history. The Yemen was mourning
Imru' al-Qays, erasing images and chewing the *qat* leaves.
Didn't you realize, friend, that we were following the Caesar of our time?

We went to the poverty-stricken paradise of the *fakirs* so as to open windows
     in the rocks.
We are besieged by tribes, friend, stricken by misfortunes.
Yet we didn't trade the bread of the trees for the enemy's loaf.

Aren't we still entitled to believe in our dreams and to doubt this homeland?

Another Damascus in Damascus

Another Damascus in Damascus, an eternal one.

I was unfair to you, friend, when you criticized my migration to a heartbeat.

Now it's my right, now after my return, to ask you in friendship:

Why did you lean on a dagger to look at me?

Why did you raise up my slopes even higher

so that my horses may fall on me?

I had hoped to carry you to the gushing spring

of the ode, to the ends of the earth. What a beauty you are!

What a beauty is Damascus if it were not for my wounds.

So let one half of your heart, friend, join one half of mine.

Let us create a strong and farseeing heart for her, for me, for you.

For another Damascus to mirror my soul in Damascus.

The Flute Cried

The flute cried. If only I could go to Damascus as an echo.

Silk weeps on the shores and passes through a sobbing cry.

Landscapes fill with tears. The flute cried and tore the sky into two women.

It divided the road and broke the heart of the sand grouse.

It divided us so we'd fall in love. O flute, we plea for mercy!

We are not as distant as the sunset. Are you crying out so as to cry in vain,

or to crush the mountain as well as Adam and Eve's apple? O shout of

    infinite silence, cry: *Damascus, my woman, I will love and I will survive.*

The flute cried. If only I could go to Damascus as an echo.

I even believe in what I don't believe. Silky tears burn away our breath.

The flute cried. If only I could cry like the flute, then I would know Damascus.

In This Hymn

In this hymn we lay a dream in the horseman's heart.

We raise his last shirt, a victory sign, and hold a key to the last door.

We enter the first sea. Peace be unto you, brother of this place that is no place.

Peace be unto your feet—shepherds won't notice your eyes twinkling in the soil.

Peace be unto your arms—the sand grouse will flutter here again.

Peace be unto your lips—prayers will flower in the field.

What can we say to the embers of your eyes?

What will absence tell your mother? He slept well? What will the invaders say?

We conquered the cloud speaking in August.

What does life say to Mahmoud Darwish?

You lived, fell in love, learned, and all those you will finally love are dead?

In this hymn we lay a dream, we raise a victory sign, we hold a key to the

    last door,

to lock ourselves in a dream. But we will survive because life is life.

from

I See What

I Want to See

1993

Translated by Munir Akash and Carolyn Forché

The Hoopoe

We have not yet come to the land of our distant star.
The poem threads us through the needle's eye
to weave the *aba* of a new horizon.
We are captives, even if our wheat grows over the fences,
and swallows rise from our broken chains.
We are captives of what we love, what we desire, and what we are.
But, among us there is a hoopoe who dictates
his letters to the olive tree of exile.
And our letters are returned for us to rewrite
what the rain has written—wild flowers on distant rocks.
An echo breaks in us and dies
in order for the journey to complete itself.
We were not basil returning in spring to our small windows.
We were not leaves for the wind to blow us back to our shores.
Here and there a clear line marks our route of wandering.
For how many years should we sacrifice our dead
to the oblivion mirrored in melodious ambiguity?
For how many years should our wounded lift
mountains of salt so that we might find the commandments?
Our letter is returned to us, and here and there
a clear line marks the shadow.

How many seas should we cross in the desert?

How many tablets should we leave behind?

How many prophets should we kill at high noon?

How many nations should we resemble before we become a tribe?

This path—our path—is a tapestry of words.

With it we mend the hem of the *aba* stretched between our solitude

and the vagrant land sleeping in our saffron dusk.

So let's be an open hand, offering our time to the gods.

I am a hoopoe, said the guide to the master of things,

searching for a lost sky.

There is nothing left of us in the wilderness

save what the wilderness kept for itself:

a skin's tatters on the thorn, a warrior's song for his homeland,

and a mouth of emptiness.

Our ruins lie ahead of us, and behind is our absurd objective.

I am a hoopoe, said the guide, and flew away in dust and beams of light.

The elders try to find a meaning for the legend and the journey:

Where did we come from?

Our ruins lie ahead of us, and behind is the willow.

From our names we come to our names

and hide our forgetfulness from our children.

Mountain goats leap out of mountain goats onto the temples.

Birds lay their eggs on strange statues.

We didn't ask why man is not born of trees

so as to be reborn in spring.

The priestesses foretold:

The obelisk shall prop up the broken horizon

and hold it from collapsing onto Time—

The outer darkness shall witness our wandering anew.

The priestesses foretold: *Kings shall be our judges.*

Our enemies will be our witnesses

and shepherds will protect our soul.

Our journey is a bridge over two rivers.

We are not born for life to erase us, or itself.

I am a hoopoe, said the guide, *and I will find*

my way to the spring when the plants wither.

We said: *We are not birds.*

He said: *You will not reach Him. All are His.*

All are in Him, and all are His manifestations.

Seek Him to find Him in Himself. He is within Himself.

We said: *We are not birds able to fly.*

He said: *My wings are time.*

Love is the fire of love, so catch fire

to free yourself from the body of place.

We asked: *Have you returned from Sheba to take us to a new Sheba?*

Our letters were returned to us, yet you were not returned

. . . you returned not.

In Greece you didn't comprehend Aristophanes.

In the city you didn't find the city.
You didn't find the tender home so as to dress us in the silk of serenity.
You didn't grasp the meaning, and the mystery of poetry obsessed you:
Fly, daughter of my feather, fly! You birds of plain and valley, fly!
Fly swiftly toward my wings, toward my voice!
There is a burning desire in us to fly into the openness of our longing!
People are birds unable to fly, O hoopoe of words.

Hatch the meaning so that birds may snatch us from words,

O child of stress and tension, when a butterfly

opens her wings and feeling overwhelms her,

fire our sounding clay so the image

of these things will be blazed by light.

Soar so that the distance between our past

and our nearest present's openness will be open—

The further we move away, the closer we come

to our reality and the boundaries of exile.

Our sole desire is to cross them.

We are the duality, heaven-earth, earth-heaven.

A boundary within a boundary surrounds us.

What is behind the boundary?

He taught Adam all the names, so that the great mystery could reveal

our journey to the mysterious.

People are birds unable to fly.

I am a hoopoe, said the guide.

Beneath us is Noah's flood, Babylon, broken corpses,

skeletons, temples, and the breath of peoples' cries

for help upon the face of the waters.

An end like a beginning, like the beginning of an end.

Soar so that the murderer forgets his victims.

Soar above us. Soar so that the Creator forgets his creature,

as well as the things and the names of things

in the creation myth that we hold in common.

—Did you know?

—I knew a volcano would shape a new image of the universe.

—But you said nothing, though you are the messenger to this earth.

—In Him there are enough ghosts to make

the lover search for his loved one in the graveyard.

He had a mother, and a southern wind to ride.

His mythic intuition was crowned with water.

On his path there was a king, a woman, and an army guarding

the desire of our two bodies against the slanderer.

We have enough desert for us to surrender

the bridle of our mirage and our clouds,

and delicate enough to yield to him the dream of our dream.

Take us. Our tongue is torn, so how can we

praise Him who is asking for praise?

His eulogy is within Him. All is within Him, and all is for all.

We admitted that we were human beings

and melted for love in this desert.

Where is our palm tree so we can identify our hearts by its dates?

God is more beautiful than the path to God.

But those who travel to nowhere have no chance of return,

to become lost again in loss.

They know that the real path leads to the beginning of the impossible path.

O hoopoe of mysteries, struggle

for our love to be worthy of our beloved.

It's an eternal journey in search of an attribute

who is nothing like Him, and who is beyond

our description and even beyond His own.

Soar with us! Nothing is left of us save our journey to him.

To Him only we complain of what we suffer on this road.

Our blood is the wine of His people, on the marble and at the banquet
    of dusk.

There is no You but You.

So, if you would, take us to You, guide us to the ungraspable land.

Take us before we whirl into deep nothingness.

Guide us one day to the trees we were

clandestinely born under so they might hide our shadows.

Guide us to the realm of our childhood,

and to doves soaring for the first time, to humble us.

Doves that forbade their chicks to fly, and they never flew.

If only . . . if only, and . . .

Perhaps we will fly one day . . .

People are birds unable to fly.

Ignorance makes the earth larger.

The earth grows smaller when we realize our ignorance,

but we are the descendants of this clay.

And fiery Satan, like us,

is trying to unveil the intimate mysteries

that he may burn us, and torch our minds.

The mind is nothing but smoke—let it be lost!

The heart is our guide, O hoopoe of mysteries,

guide us to vanish in His vanishing.

Soar with us and land, that we may bid farewell to our mother,

waiting eons for our horses.

Let her die embracing light or let her live

for Nishapur, a widow enchanting our nights.

She "wants in the pantheon of gods no God but Allah."

Take us. Real love is loving what cannot be possessed.

With the echo of the flutes, the lover sent to his beloved

the mare of his exile and thus shortened the road.

I am her "she," and she is the "I" slipping

from despair to the hope that changes into despair.

My roads do not lead to her door.

My "I" has flown away. For there is no "I" but "I."

My roads do not lead to her doors and the road of nations

does not lead to the same old springs.

We said: *Heaven's messages will be completed when we cross*

this archipelago and free the captives from the tablets.

So, let this void be crowned,

for our human nature to complete its migration.

What are these flutes seeking in the forests?

We are the strangers and we, the people of the deserted temple,

have been abandoned on our white horses searching for our last station,

reeds sprouting from our bodies and comets crisscrossing over our heads.

There is no place on earth where we haven't pitched our tent of exile.

Are we the skin of this earth? What are the words searching for within us

when the words, in the underworld, brought us to trial in the court of insight

and built temples to tame the wild beast of their isolation with icons

    and cornets?

Our ruins lie ahead of us, here as well as there.

The priestesses foretold:

The city in ancient China worships its ancestors.

The priestesses foretold:

The grandfather takes his throne with him to his holy tomb,

and takes girls as wives and prisoners-of-war as guards.

The priestesses foretold:

Divinity and humanity in ancient India were twins.

The priestesses foretold what all beings foretold:

You also will be what He is.

But we didn't climb our fig tree

so the southern invaders could hang us on it.

Are we the skin of the earth?

We gnawed on stones to open a space for jasmine.

We took refuge in God from His guards, and from wars.

We believed in what we learned from words.

Poetry was exhaled from the fruit of our nights,

and from herding our goats on their way to pasture.

Dawn was blue, tender and dewy,

and our dreams were modest, the size of our houses:

we see honey on the carobs and gather it.

We dream that the sesame seeds on the terraces

are heaped up, and we sift them.

We see in the dream what we then face at dawn.

The lover's scarf was the dream.

Yet we did not raise our fig tree

so the southern invaders could hang us upon it.

I am a hoopoe, said the guide, and flew away with our words.

We witnessed the flood, yet we didn't take off our earthly clothes.

We witnessed the flood, but we didn't start the war against the self.

We witnessed the flood, yet we didn't harvest the barley of our
   golden plains.

We witnessed the flood, but we didn't polish our stones with
   rams' horn.

We witnessed the flood, yet we didn't give up our desire for apples.

Our broken-hearted mother will give birth to other brothers of our flesh,

neither of chestnut trunks nor of iron.

Our broken-hearted mother will give birth

to brothers, to build an exile for the song.

Our broken-hearted mother will give birth to brothers

to dwell, if they like, under palm fronds,

or on the backs of our horses.

Our broken-hearted mother will give birth to brothers

and they will crown their Abel on a throne of mud.

Our journey to oblivion has been endlessly prolonged.

The veil before us obscures every other veil.

Maybe traveling only half the road will lead us to a road of clouds.

Perhaps, O hoopoe of mysteries, we are nothing but ghosts searching

    for ruins.

He said: *To follow me, take off your bodies, and abandon this earth-mirage.*

To follow me, abandon your names and don't ask for an answer.

The answer is the road, and the road is nothing but vanishing into fog.

We said: *Did Al-'Attar put a spell on you and obsess you with poetry?*

He said: *He spoke to me and disappeared into the belly of the valley of love.*

We asked: *Did Al-Ma'arri gaze upon the valley of knowledge?*

He said: *His path was futile.*

And Ibn Sina, we asked, did he answer the question? Did he see you?

He said: *I see with the heart, not with philosophy.*

Are you a Sufi, then? we asked.

He answered: *I am a hoopoe. I want nothing.*

I want only to have no want.

And he disappeared into the realm of his longing.

You have tortured us, O love.

In vain you drive us from journey to journey.

You have tossed us away from our kin,

from our water and air, and you have ruined us.

You have emptied the sunset of sunset.

You've robbed us of our first words

and looted the peach tree of our days.

You have stripped us of our days.

O love, you have tortured us and sacked our lives.

You have tossed us away from everything

and then taken cover behind Autumn's leaves.

You sacked our lives, O love!

You've left not a thing to guide us to you,

or whose shadow we can kiss.

Leave in the wheat fields of our souls one grain of your love.

Do not break the cosmic glass prison of our supplication.

Do not worry. Do not raise a hue and cry.

Calm down, so that we may witness

the cosmic wedding of the elements, an offering to you.

Come closer so that, at least once, we can comprehend:

Are we worthy to be the slaves of your mysterious ecstasy?

Don't dissipate what remains of our ruined sky.

O love you have tortured us.

O blessed love that disperses us and leads us toward our thundering fate.

Neither this fate nor the mouth of the river is ours.

Before our eyes, life is the wind-tossed leaves

of an old cypress leading us from longing to longing.

O love, how bitterly you tortured us and estranged us from our very self!

You have stripped us even of our names, O love!

The drunken hoopoe said: *To fly you should fly.*

We said: *We are nothing but lovers*

and we are tired of love's whiteness,

and we are filled with craving for a mother, a land and a father.

Are we the people we were, the people we will become?

He said: *Be united on all paths and become breath*

so that you may reach Him who is beyond the senses.

Every heart is a cosmos of mysteries.

To fly you should fly. We are nothing but lovers, we said,

and we have died time after time after time, and have been exultant.

Longing is the place of exile. Our love is a place of exile.

Our wine is a place of exile

and a place of exile is the history of this heart.

How many times have we told the fragrance of the place

to be still so we can rest and sleep?

How many times have we told the trees

of the place to wipe off the invader's mask

so we might find a place? Nowhere is the place

that distances its soul from its history.

A place of exile is the soul

that distances us from our land and takes us to our love.

A place of exile is the soul

that distances us from our soul and takes us to the stranger.

Is there a sword that hasn't yet been sheathed in our flesh?

To relinquish our dream, our brother-enemies

have saddled the horses of the enemies, that they may exit from our dreams.

The past is a place of exile,

we tried to pick up the prunes of our exultance from that dead summer.

Thought is a place of exile:

we saw our future just behind our windows.

To reach it, we broke through the walls of our present,

and it became a past in the shield of an ancient soldier.

Poetry is a place of exile.

We dream and forget where we were when we wake.

Do we deserve a gazelle?

O hoopoe of mysteries, take us to our endless tomorrow!

Hitch our time to the horizon of this vastness and soar with us.

Nature is nothing but spirit, and the earth seems, from here,

a breast aroused by that sublime coming.

The wind is our chariot, O birds.

To fly you should fly. Nature is nothing but spirit.

Enchanted by the yellow hand, flutter about

your sun, so you can melt, then turn, after your burning

to that land, your land.

You will light up the tunnel of the unthinkable questions

about this existence and about the brief wall of time.

Nature is nothing but spirit. And the body's last dance is spirit.

To fly, you should fly higher than flying . . . above your sky,

higher than the perennial love,

than holiness and divinity and passion.

Free yourselves of questions about the beginning and destiny.

The universe is smaller than a butterfly's wing

in the boundless expanse of the heart.

We met in a grain of wheat,

then parted in the loaf and on the roads of life.

But who are we, in this hymn, to roof the desert with pouring rain?

Or free the living from their graves?

O birds, flap the wings of your dazzling and fly away on storms of silk.

Fly in a rapture like ours. The cosmic resonance is urging you. Fly!

Yours is the radiance of vision.

We will alight onto ourselves

and return if we should awaken.

We will visit a time insufficient to satisfy

either our exultation or rites of resurrection.

But who are we in this hymn

to meet its opposite in time, as a door in a wall?

For what use is our thought if not for mankind?

We are of fire and we are of light.

I am hoopoe, said the guide.

We are a flock of birds, we said:

Words are sick of us and we are sick of our loss,

of the echo and our thirst for words.

How long should we fly?

Said the drunken hoopoe:

Our destination is the horizon of this expanse.

We said: *What's beyond this expanse?*

He said: *An expanse after an expanse after an expanse.*

But we are tired, we said. And he said:

You will not find a pine tree to rest near.

In vain you strive to land. To soar you should soar.

We said: *Tomorrow we'll fly again.*

That land is a full breast milked by that cloud

and gold fluttering in azure light around our houses.

All of this was there and we were unaware?

We'll return, when we return, to see her!

With the eyes of our hoopoe casting its spell over our insight.

Peace be upon her!

Peace is hers. Hers is the cosmic bed of clouds and visions.

She lies asleep on an arm of water.

She sleeps—an image of herself and us.

She has a small moon, a servant combing

her shadow, and flickering through our hearts

in fear of exile and the fate imposed on us by myths.

Darkness kindles him with light, so that he guards

himself in that realm of miracles.

Is it here that speech was born for mud to become man?

We knew her to forget her and to forget

our childhood's fishing around her navel.

Can we see clearly from this distance?

How the days were horses for us to race on strings of words!

How the rivers were flutes and we were unaware!

How many of our angels were imprisoned in marble

while we were unaware! How many times Egypt and Syria went astray!

The land has another land, and our hoopoe was imprisoned there.

The land has a spirit for the wind to blow itself away.

Noah didn't leave us all his messages.

When Christ walked in Galilee our wounds rejoiced in happiness.

But here the doves are the words of our dead.

Here, the ruins of Babylon are a birthmark

On the flesh of our legacy.

The fruits of this flesh drift in the galaxy's watery sphere flowing into an eternity embedded in our eulogies.

Then it travels self-ward,

a mother wrapping us in the naked invincible compassion.

She covers up the harm we did to the lungs, and the fire of her rose.

She covers up the war of our legacy

and what the scythe did to those tender plants

along the shores of the sacred *mons*.

Our mother is our mother, mother of the Athenians,

mother of the ancient Persians,

Mother of Plato, Zarathustra, Plotinus, mother of Suhrawardi.

She is the cosmic mother.

Each child is a master in his mother's lap.

For she is the beginning and the end.

She is what she is,

she is birth if she wishes, or inviolable death.

O mother, you nurtured us and devoured us to feed our children.

When will the weaning come?

O spider of love, death is a murderer.

How we love you! O have mercy on us.

Don't kill us again and don't give birth to serpents near the Tigris.

Tuck us into your belt and ride gazelles through the night.

We settle in the wind.

Lure us to you like the unfortunate partridge

is lured to the net, and embrace us.

Were you yourself before our migration and were we unaware?

Love transforms us. We become an ode opening

its windows to be recited and finished by doves.

We become a meaning that returns sap

to invisible trees on our souls' embankments.

Fly then, O birds, in the village squares of my heart, fly!

For what use is our thought if not for mankind?

We are of clay and light.

Did you recognize the crown above your head?

It's my mother's tomb.

A festival crowns my head as I fly carrying secrets and news.

He is a hoopoe, and he is the guide and what is in him is also in us.

Time hangs a bell for him over the valleys.

But in dreams, time shatters and place closes in.

What do you see? What do you see in that distant shape of the shadow?

The shadow of his image stretches above us.

Let's soar to see him. There is no "he" but "he."

O heart—my mother, my sister and wife, flood with life to see him!

To our hoopoe, thrones of water rising

through the drought, and oak trees growing tall

to water the grove's color lifted by breeze onto the horse of dawn,

to water the echo of creation's grace,

as it is cherished in the gardens of memory,

to water the scent of the lover on marble

that makes us thirsty and drunk,

to water the sting of the moment of illumination

when we are split in two: human and bird.

And to him, our hoopoe, horses of water

emerging beneath the drought, and the mace rising higher.

To him . . . to our hoopoe, a time to fly and a tongue he once had.

To him . . . to our hoopoe, a homeland he carries as messages to heaven.

He tried every divine message to lead creation on the path of God

and he suffered every possible love,

breaking through one love after another.

He is a life-long traveler.

Who are you in this hymn? I am the guide.

He is a life-long traveler.

Who are you in this hymn? I am the journey.

O heart—my mother, my sister and wife,

flood with life so you can embrace the impossible,

and you see it, then our hoopoe flew away.

Are we ourselves? Trees grow in our tracks,

and a beautiful moon lights our travels.

We have life there in others' lives.

But we are forced to live in orphaned Samarkand.

No king of our ancestors will be crowned again.

The flute is the cry of our inherited days.

Its nearest is the most distant.

We do not take from the rains any more than ivy vines take.

We are now who we were before.

And we are forced to return to the inhospitable myths

where we have no place.

We couldn't milk the ewes near our houses, or fill the days with our hymn.

Our temples are there. Here we have a god praised by his martyr.

And ours is the night-musk flower clutched by an unwelcoming time.

We have life there in the lives of others.

Here we have wheat and olive oil.

We haven't cut our tent out of willows.

We haven't made gods out of sulphur to be worshipped by invaders.

Everything was prepared: our names, broken in a clay jar . . .

Our women's tears, old mulberry stains on their clothes.

Old hunting rifles—

An old forgotten celebration.

Wilderness is teeming with the relics of human absence

as if we were here.

Here are enough tools to pitch a tent above the winds.

No tattoo left by the flood

in the crevasse of the mountain bordered in green.

Yet among us one thousand different peoples passed between songs

   and spears.

We came back, only to realize that we returned from an unwanted absence.

We have yet to try life, and the salt that didn't bestow its eternal life upon us.

We still have steps no one before us has ever walked. So fly,

fly, then, O birds in the squares of the heart, fly!

Flock with our hoopoe, and fly!

And fly, just to fly.

from

Why Have You

Left the Horse Alone?

1995

Translated by Amira El-Zein and edited by Munir Akash and Carolyn Forché

I See My Ghost Coming from Afar

Like a balcony, I gaze upon whatever I desire.
I see my friends bearing the evening mail—wine, bread,
a few novels and records.

I gaze upon a seagull and troop trucks arriving
to change the trees of this place.

I gaze upon the dog of the neighbor who left
Canada a year and a half ago.

I gaze upon the name of Al-Mutanabbi
journeying from Tiberias to Egypt
on a horse of song.

I gaze upon the Persian flower
leaping the iron fence.

Like a balcony, I gaze upon whatever I desire.

I gaze upon trees guarding the night from the night
and the sleep of those who would wish me death.

~

I gaze upon the wind chasing the wind
so that it might find a home in the wind.

I gaze upon a woman basking in herself.

I gaze upon the procession of ancient prophets
climbing barefoot to Jerusalem
and I ask: *will there be a new prophet for this new time?*

Like a balcony, I gaze upon whatever I desire.

I gaze upon my image hurrying away from itself,
ascending the stone stairs, my mother's scarf in her hand
flapping in the wind: what might happen if I were a child again?
And if you came back to me, and I came back to you?

I gaze upon the trunk of the olive tree that hid Zechariah.
I gaze upon the extinct words in the Arabic dictionary.

I gaze upon the Persians, the Romans, the Sumerians,
and the new refugees . . .

I gaze upon the necklace of one of Tagore's women *fakirs*
as it is crushed by the carriage of a handsome emir.

~

I gaze upon a hoopoe tired of his king's blame.

I gaze upon the unseen:
What will come—what will come after the ashes?

I gaze upon my body frightened from afar.

Like a balcony, I gaze upon whatever I desire.

I gaze upon my language.
A little absence is enough for Aeschylus to open the door to peace,
for Antonio to make a brief speech at the outbreak of war,
for me to hold a woman's hand in my hand,
to embrace my freedom,
and for my body to begin its ebb and tide anew.

Like a balcony, I gaze upon whatever I desire.

I gaze upon my ghost approaching from afar.

A Cloud in My Hands

They saddled the horses.
They didn't know why,
but they saddled the horses in the plains.

The place was ready for his birth:
a hill covered by his ancestor's basil,
with views to the east and west.
God's olive trees rising with the language,
and an azure smoke wafting through this day
dedicated only to God.
March is the most coddled child of the months.
March combs its cotton over the almond trees.
March offers a feast of mallow in the churchyard.
March is the floor of night for the swallow,
for a woman ready to cry out in the wilderness
and grow tall with the oaks.

A child is now born, and his cry pierces through the cracks of this place.

At the foot of the stairs of the house we bid farewell.
They said the wariness of my cry was not in harmony
with the recklessness of the plants.

~

Rain was in my cry. Did it hurt my brothers
when I said I saw angels in the house playing with the wolf?
I don't recall their names.
I don't recall their manner of speaking,
or the lightness of their flight.

My friends flutter in the night, leaving without a trace.
Shall I tell my mother the truth?
I have other brothers who place a moon on my balcony,
and weave for me a wreath of flowers.

They saddled the horses.
They didn't know why
and yet they saddled the horses at the end of night.

Seven blades of wheat are enough for a banquet in summer.
Seven blades of wheat in my hands.
In each blade, a field of wheat.
My father drew water from his well saying, do not go dry.
He took me by the hand to show me how I grew like purslane.
I walk on the lip of the well: I have two moons,
one in the sky, the other swimming in the water.
I have two moons.

~

Certain of the truth of the divine messages,

like their ancestors, they melted the swords' iron into ploughs.

The sword does not mend what summer ruins, they said.

And they prayed and prayed.

They sang their eulogies to nature.

Yet they saddled their horses

to dance the horse dance in the silver of night.

A cloud in my hand wounds me.

I don't want more from the earth than this land,

the scent of cardamom and straw

between my father and the horse.

A cloud in my hand wounds me,

and yet I don't want more from the sun than

the orange seed, more than the golden flow

of the call to prayer.

They saddled the horses,

they didn't know why,

and yet they saddled the horses

at the end of night, and they waited

for a ghost to emerge between the cracks of this place.

The Kindhearted Villagers

I did not yet know my mother's way of life,
nor her family's, when the ships came in from the sea.
I knew the scent of tobacco in my grandfather's *aba,*
and ever since I was born here, all at once, like a domestic animal,
I knew the eternal smell of coffee.

We, too, cry when we fall to the earth's rim.
Yet we don't preserve our voices in old jars.
We don't hang a mountain goat's horns on the wall,
and we don't make of our dust a kingdom.
Our dreams do not gaze upon other people's grapevines.
They don't break the rule.

My name had no feathers, so I couldn't fly beyond midday.
April's warmth was like the balalaikas of our passing visitors.
It caused us to fly like doves.
My first fright: the charm of a girl who seduced me into
smelling milk on her knees, but I fled that meal's sting!

We, too, have our mystery when the sun falls from white poplars.
We are overwhelmed by a desire to cry for one who has died for nothing,

and by an eagerness to visit Babylon or a mosque in Damascus.
In the eternal saga of pain, we are the teardrop in the dove's cooing.

We are kindhearted villagers and we don't regret our words.
Our names, like our days, are the same.
Our names don't reveal us. We infiltrate the talk of our guests.
We have things to tell the woman stranger
about the land she embroiders on her scarf
with the pinions of our returning sparrows!

When the ships came in from the sea,
this place was held together only by trees.
We were feeding our cows in their enclosures
and organizing our days in closets made by our own hands.
We were coaxing the horse, and beckoning to the wandering star.

We, too, boarded the ships, entertained by
the radiance of the emerald in our olive at night,
and by dogs barking at a fleeting moon above the church tower,
yet we were unafraid.
For our childhood had not boarded with us.
We were satisfied with a song.
Soon we'll go back to our house
when the ships unload their excess cargo.

The Owl's Night

There is, here, a present not embraced by the past.
When we reached the last of the trees, we knew we were unable to pay attention.
And when we returned to the ships, we saw absence piling up its chosen objects
and pitching its eternal tent around us.

There is, here, a present not embraced by the past.
A silken thread is drawn out of mulberry trees
forming letters on the page of night.
Only the butterflies cast light upon our boldness
in plunging into the pit of strange words.
Was that condemned man my father?
Perhaps I can handle my life here.
Perhaps I can now give birth to myself
and choose different letters for my name.

There is, here, a present, sitting in an empty kitchen
gazing at the tracks of those crossing the river on reeds.
A present polishing the flutes with its wind.

Perhaps speech could become transparent, so we could
see open windows in it, and perhaps time could hurry along with us,
carrying our tomorrow in its luggage.

There is, here, a timeless present, and here no one can find anyone.
No one remembers how we went out the door like a gust of wind,
and at what hour we fell from yesterday, and then
yesterday shattered on the tiles
in shards for others to reassemble into mirrors
reflecting their images over ours.

There is, here, a placeless present.
Perhaps I can handle my life and cry out in the owl's night:
Was this condemned man my father who burdens me with his history?
Perhaps I will be transformed within my name, and will choose
my mother's words and way of life, exactly as they should be.
Thus, she could cajole me each time salt touched my blood,
and give me food each time a nightingale bit me in the mouth.

There is, here, a transient present.
Here, strangers hang their rifles on the olive's branches,
to prepare their dinner in haste out of tin cans
and rush hurriedly to their trucks.

The Everlasting Indian Fig

Where are you taking me, father?
Where the wind blows, son.

While leaving the plains where Bonaparte's soldiers
erected a hill to watch the shadows on ancient Acre's wall,
a father says to his son: *Do not be afraid.*
Do not be afraid of the whir of bullets.
Hold fast to the ground.
You will be saved and we will climb a mountain in the north
and come back when the soldiers return to their families in distant lands.

—And who will live in the house after us, O my father?
—It will remain as it is.

He felt for his keys as he would his limbs, and his mind was at rest.
And he said while crossing a fence of thorns:
O my son, remember! Here on the thorn of an Indian fig,
the English crucified your father for two nights
but he never confessed. You will grow up, my son,
and tell those who inherited their rifles
the legacy of our blood on their iron.

~

—Why have you left the horse alone?
—To keep the house company, O my son,
for houses perish if their inhabitants go away.

Eternity opens its doors from afar to travelers at night.
Wolves in the wilderness howl at a frightened moon,
and a father says to his son: *Be strong like your grandfather!*
Climb the last hill of oaks with me.
Remember, son: here the last inkishari fell from his war mule—
So remain defiant until our return.

—When will that be, O my father?
—Tomorrow. Perhaps in two days.

It was a heedless tomorrow that chewed on the wind
behind them on the long winter nights.
Joshua's soldiers built their fortress with the stones of their houses.
Breathless on the road to Cana: here our Lord passed one day.
Here he transformed water into wine.
Here he said many things about love.
O my son, remember tomorrow.
And remember the fortresses of the crusades
eaten by April's grasses after the soldiers left.

The Lute of Ismael

A horse dancing on two strings—
thus Ismael's fingers listen to his blood,
and villages bloom like red anemones in the cadence.
There is no night there and no day.
A heavenly rapture transports us,
and the earth hastens back to the primordial.
Alleluia!
Alleluia!
Everything will begin again!

Our neighbor in the oak forest is the owner of an old lute.
He carries time with him disguised as a mad singer.
The war was over, and before they could give birth to the phoenix,
the ashes of our village, as expected, vanished in a black cloud,
and night's blood had not yet dried on the shirts of the dead.
Plants didn't grow from the soldiers' helmets
as one might expect in oblivion.
Alleluia!
Alleluia!
Everything will begin again.

~

Like a desert, space recedes from time

the distance needed for a poem to explode.

Ismael used to come down among us at night

and sing: *O stranger, I am the stranger*

and you are part of me, O stranger.

The desert vanishes in the words

and the words ignore the power of things:

O lute, give me back what has been lost,

and sacrifice me over it.

Alleluia!

Alleluia!

Everything will begin again!

Within us, meaning breathes,

and we fly from one plateau

to another made of marble

and we run between two blue bottomless pits.

Our dreams never wake, nor do the guardians of this place

leave Ismael's space. No earth here, no heaven.

A collective rapture transports us before

that isthmus created by two strings.

Ismael, sing for us, that everything may become possible

at the door of being!
Alleluia!
Alleluia!
Everything will begin again.

With the lute of Ismael, the Sumerian wedding
arrives at the sword's edge, where
there is neither life nor death.
A lust for creation seizes us:
water flows from a string,
from two strings, a flame darts
from three strings, a woman radiates
the heavens—illumination—
Sing, Ismael, that meaning may soar
at dusk as a bird soars over Athens
between two histories.
Sing for a funeral on a feast day.
Alleluia!
Alleluia!
Everything will begin again.

The foreign horses pass beneath the poem.
Carriages pass over the shoulders of prisoners.
Beneath the poem, oblivion and the Hyksos pass.

The lords of time, the philosophers,

sad Imru' al-Qays—they all pass beneath the poem,

toward a future thrown against Caesar's door.

The even more recent past, as did Tamerlane, passes beneath the poem.

The prophets pass and listen to Ismael singing:

O stranger, I am a stranger and you are like me.

O stranger, far from home, go back.

O lute, bring back what is lost, and sacrifice over you

from jugular to jugular.

Alleluia!

Alleluia!

Everything will begin again.

The Strangers' Picnic

I know the house from the bundle of sage.
The first window is open toward the butterflies,
—blue, red. I know the course of the clouds
and in which well they await the village women in summer.
I know what the dove means when it lays its eggs on the rifle's muzzle.
I know who opens the door to the jasmine tree
as it makes our dreams blossom for the evening's guests.

The strangers' carriage has not yet arrived.

No one has arrived. So leave me there as you leave
your greeting at the door of the house, for me or for the others.
You pay no heed to who hears it first.
Leave me there, talking to myself:
Was I lonely—alone like a soul in a body,
when you said to me once: *I love you both,*
you and the water? Thus the water shone in everything
as if a guitar had been crying.

The strangers' guitar has not yet arrived.

~

Let us be kindhearted! Take me to the sea at dusk.

Let me hear what the sea tells you when it returns to itself in peace.

I won't change. I will embrace a wave and say:

Take me to the sea again.

This is what the fearful do:

when a burning star torments them, they go to the sea.

The strangers' song has not yet arrived.

I know the house from its waving scarves.

The first doves weep on my shoulders,

and beneath the sky of the Gospels

a child runs for no reason.

The water flows, the cypress flows,

the wind flows in the wind

and the earth flows within itself.

I said: *Don't be in a rush when you leave the house.*

Nothing forbids this place from waiting a little here

while you put on the day and shoes of the wind.

The strangers' myth has not yet arrived.

No one has arrived. Leave me there

as you would leave a myth with any person who sees you

until he cries and rushes into himself, afraid of happiness:

~

I love you so, you are so much yourself!

He is so afraid of his soul:

no "I" now but she. She is now within me.

And no "she" now but only my fragile "I."

At the end of this song, how much I fear that my dream

may not see its dream in her.

No one has arrived.

Perhaps the strangers lost the way to the strangers' picnic.

The Raven's Ink

You have your retreat in the solitude of a carob tree,
O bell of dusk with the dark voice!
Now what do they ask of you?
In Adam's garden you searched, that a restless killer
may bury his brother, and descended
into your darkness, where the corpse was exposed to the four winds.
Then you went about your work,
as absence goes about its own preoccupations.
Be alert, raven! Our resurrection will be postponed.

No night is long enough for us to dream twice.
There is only one door to our heaven.
Where will the end come from?
We are the descendents of the beginning.
We only see the beginning.
So come out of the origin of night
as a priest, and preach with your always
echoing voice the human void surrounding you!
You are accused of what is within us.
Here, before you, is the first blood of our line.

Fly from the new house of Cain

the way the mirage left the ink of your feathers, O raven!

I have taken refuge in the night of your voice.

My absence is roaming among the shadows, and tugging at me.

I cling to a bull's horn.

It was a battle with the unseen, a push and pull, a back and forth,

a down and up with a ghost, dangling like a ripe eggplant.

Is that you then? What do they still want from us

after having stolen my words from yours, after

having slept in my dream with their weapons always at their sides?

I was not a ghost, so they followed my footsteps.

Be my second brother.

I am Abel, and the soil returns me to you

as a carob tree, so you settle on my branch, raven!

You and I are one in words.

We belong to the same book.

The ashes upon you are mine,

and in the shadow we are

the only two witnesses, victims,

two short poems about nature

waiting for the devastation to finish its feast.

~

And the Qur'an illuminates you:

Then God sent a raven who scratched the ground

to show him how to hide the vile body of his brother.

Woe is me! said he. Was I not even able to be as this raven?

As the Qur'an illuminates you,

search for our resurrection, O raven, and soar.

Like the Letter "N" in the Qur'an

East of the springs, in a forest of olives,
my grandfather embraced his forsaken shadow.
No mythical grass sprouted on his shadow,
no lilac cloud rained upon that land.

In his shattered dream, the earth is a robe
woven by the sumac needle.
My grandfather awakened to gather herbs from his vineyard
that was buried under the black road.

He taught me the Qur'an in the basil garden
east of the well:
We descended from Adam and Eve
who were in the paradise of oblivion.
O grandfather, I am the last of the living in this desert, so let us return.

No one guards my grandfather's name
bordered by a sea and a desert,
and both deny my grandfather and his sons
hovering now around the letter "N."
In *surat* al-Rahman of the Qur'an,
O God, be my witness!

~

As he was born of himself
and buried within himself close to hell,
let him bestow upon the phoenix
a little of his secret's fire
so she may kindle the lights
in the temple after him.

East of the springs, in a forest of olives,
my grandfather embraced his forsaken shadow.
No sun rises on his shadow, no shadow sets upon him.
My grandfather is forever beyond.

Ivory Combs

Clouds descend blue from the citadel to the alleys.
The silk shawl flutters and the dove flock lifts.
On the pond's face the sky wanders a little and then flies off.
My soul, like a worker bee, flies through the alleys.
The sea eats her bread, the bread of Acre,
and for five thousand years the sea
polishes its ring and presses its cheek to her cheek
in an endless wedding rite.

The poem says: *Let us wait for the window to fall*
on the tour guide's brochure.

I enter from its stone embrace the way waves enter timelessness.
I cross from one age to another as if from room to room.
I see in my self's time certain familiar things:
the mirrors of the daughter of Canaan, ivory combs,
an Assyrian soup bowl, the sword of the soldier
who guards his sleeping Persian master.
And falcons fly from mast to mast through the fleet.

Would that I had a different present,
I would hold the keys to my past.

And would that I had a past within me,
I would possess all tomorrows.

Mysterious is my journey in the long alley,
leading to an obscure moon above the copper market.
Here is a palm tree
that carries the tower instead of me.
Here is the obsession with a song
through which I convey a repeated tragedy.
Here, the imagination trudges intimately through the dust—
a hungry peddler, door-to-door.
As if I had nothing to do with my own fate
to be decided later at Julius Caesar's jubilee.

My beloved and I drink the waters of delight
from the same cloud and alight on the same jar.

I anchored at this port only because my mother lost her scarves here—
but I have no legends here.
I don't exchange gods, nor do I negotiate with them.
I have no stories from here to fill my memory with barley,
and the names of guardians waiting behind my back
for Thotmes' dawn. I have no sword here, no story
which would permit me to repudiate my mother,

who, at the time of departure, made me fly her scarves,
cloud after cloud, over the old port of Acre.

But other things will happen.
Henry will lie to Qalawoon
and soon red clouds will rise over the palms.

The Death of the Phoenix

In the songs we sing there is a flute.
In the flute that dwells within us there is a fire.
In the fire that we kindle there is a green phoenix.
And in the elegy of the phoenix I can't tell my ashes
apart from your dust.

A lilac cloud is enough to hide the hunter's tent from us.
So walk on the water like the Lord, she said:
No desert is reflected in what I remember of you,
henceforth the roses that blossom from your ruined house
will have no enemies!

The water was a ring around the high mountain.
And Tiberias, the backyard for the first paradise.
I said: *The image of the world has been perfected*
in your two green eyes.
She said: *My prince and my prisoner,*
put my wines into your jars!

The two strangers who burned within us are those
who wanted to murder us only moments ago,

who will come back to their swords after a while,
who will ask: *Who are you?*
—We are two shadows of our past lives here,
and two names for the wheat that sprouts
from the bread of battles.

I don't want to return home now,
the way the Crusaders returned.
I am all this silence between two fronts:
gods on one side, those who invent their names on the other.
I am the shadow who walks on water.
I am the witness and the thing witnessed,
the worshipper and the temple
in the land of both your siege and mine.

Be my lover between two wars waged in the mirror, she said.
I don't want to return now to the fortress of my father's house.
Take me to your vineyard.
Let me meet your mother.
Perfume me with basil water.
Arrange me on silver dishes, comb me,
imprison me in your name,
let love kill me.

Wed me, marry me to the agrarian life,
teach me the flute, burn within me to be born
like the phoenix from both my fire and yours!

Something resembling a phoenix wept and bled
before falling into the water close to the hunter's tent.

What's the use of your waiting, or mine?

Poetic Regulations

The stars had only one task: they taught me how to read.
They taught me I had a language in heaven
and another language on earth.
Who am I? Who am I?
I don't want to answer yet.
May a star fall into itself,
and may a forest of chestnut trees rise in the night
toward the Milky Way with me, and may it say:
Remain here!

The poem is "above" and can teach me whatever it wishes.
It can teach me to open a window
and to manage my household in between legends.
It can wed me to itself for a while.

My father is "below," carrying a thousand-year olive tree
that is neither from the East nor the West.
Let him rest from the conquerors for a while,
and be tender with me, and gather iris and lily for me.

~

The poem leaves me and heads for a port whose sailors love wine
and never return twice to the same woman.
They have neither regrets nor longing for anything!

I haven't died of love yet, but a mother sees in her son's eyes
the fear carnations harbor for the vase.
She cries to ward off something before it happens.
She cries for me to return alive from destiny's road
and live here.

The poem is neither here nor there, and with a girl's breast
it can illuminate the nights.
With the glow of an apple it fills two bodies with light
and with a gardenia's breath it can revive a homeland!

The poem is in my hands, and can run stories through her hands.
But ever since I embraced the poem, I squandered my soul
and then asked: *Who am I? Who am I?*

Excerpts from the Byzantine Odes of Abu Firas

An echo rebounding: a wide street in the echo.

Footsteps alternating with the sound of coughing.

Slowly, ever so slowly, they draw near to the door,

then away from the door.

Our families will visit us tomorrow. Thursday is visiting day.

Our shadow is at the gate, and our sun is in the baskets of fruit.

A mother reprimands the prison guard:

Why have you spilled our coffee onto the grass, you mischief maker?

The salt breathes the sea; the sea, the salt.

My prison cell grows by a hair to make room for the song of a dove.

O dove, fly to Aleppo with my Byzantine ode

and take my greeting to my kinsman.

An echo of the echo.

This echo has an iron ladder, a transparency, and a dew.

It's teeming with those who climb to their dawn

and those who descend from holes in the sky to their graves.

Take me with you to my language, I said.

For what is the good of mankind's remaining in the Ode?

As for the drums, they float on the skin of the words like foam.

The echo enlarged my prison cell so that it became a balcony

like the dress of the young girl who accompanied me for no reason to the train and said: *My father doesn't like you. My mother does.*

Beware of the coming Sodom, and don't wait for me on Thursday morning.

I don't like sensuality, for it darkens the nuances of meaning in my cells

and leaves my body lonely and hollow, haunted by the first forests.

There is a room in the echo like the room of my prison cell,

a room where one talks to the self.

My cells is my image. I found no one around

to share my morning coffee.

There is no seat to share my solitude this evening,

no light to share my confusion in my quest for wisdom.

Let me be what the horses in their forays wish me to be:

Let me be a prince or a prisoner: or let me die.

My cell becomes one street, two streets. And this echo

comes from that echo, whether it remains or dies away.

I will come out of these walls a free man,

like a ghost when he floats freely out of himself.

I will go to Aleppo.

Dove, fly with my Byzantine ode

to my kinsman, and take him this greeting of dew.

The Dreamers Pass from One Sky to Another

. . . And we left our childhood to the butterfly
when we left a few drops of olive oil on the stair
but we forgot to greet the mint everywhere
and we forgot to secretly greet our tomorrow.
The ink of midday was white
were it not for the butterfly's book fluttering around us.

Butterfly! sister of yourself, be what you desire
before my longing, and after.
But let me be a brother to your wing, that my madness might remain fevered.
Butterfly, born of yourself,
don't let others decide my fate. Don't abandon me.

From one sky to another the dreamers pass—
the butterfly's attendants carry mirrors of water.
We could be what we should be.
From one sky to another the dreamers pass.

The butterfly spins her garment on a needle of light, to decorate her comedy.
The butterfly is born of herself and dances in the flame of her tragedy.

~

Half phoenix, what touched her touched us:
an obscure similarity between light and fire—and between two paths.
No. Our love is neither foolishness nor wisdom.
And thus, from one sky to another the dreamers pass and pass and
   pass forever.

The butterfly is water longing to fly. It filters
from the sweat of young girls and grows into a cloud of memory.
The butterfly is what the poem doesn't say.
Her very lightness breaks words, as dreams break dreamers.

Let it be so! Let our tomorrow be present with us.
Let our yesterday be present with us.
Let today be present in the feast of this day
set for the butterfly's celebration,
and let the dreamers pass from one sky to another.

From one sky to another the dreamers pass.

A Rhyme for the Odes (Mu'allaqat)

No one guided me to myself. I am the guide.

Between desert and sea, I am my own guide to myself.

Born of language on the road to India between two small tribes,

adorned by the moonlight of ancient faiths and an impossible peace,

compelled to guard the periphery of a Persian neighborhood

and the great obsession of the Byzantines,

so that the heaviness of time lightens over the Arab's tent.

Who am I? This is a question that others ask, but has no answer.

I am my language, I am an ode, two odes, ten. This is my language.

I am my language. I am words' writ: *Be! Be my body!*

And I become an embodiment of their timbre.

I am what I have spoken to the words: *Be the place where*

my body joins the eternity of the desert.

Be, so that I may become my words.

No land on earth bears me. Only my words bear me,

a bird born from me who builds a nest in my ruins

before me, and in the rubble of the enchanting world around me.

I stood on a wind, and my long night was without end.

This is my language, a necklace of stars around the necks

of my loved ones. They emigrated.

They carried the place and emigrated, they carried time and emigrated.

They lifted their fragrances from their bowls.

They took their bleak pastures and emigrated.

They took the words. The ravaged heart left with them.

Will the echo, this echo, this white, sonorous mirage

hold a name whose hoarseness fills the unknown

and whom departure fills with divinity?

The sky opened a window for me. I looked and found nothing

save myself outside itself, as it has always been,

and my desert-haunted visions.

My steps are wind and sand, my world is my body

and what I can hold onto.

I am the traveler and also the road.

Gods appear to me and disappear.

We don't linger upon what is to come.

There is no tomorrow in this desert, save what we saw yesterday,

so let me brandish my ode to break the cycle of time,

and let there be beautiful days!

How much past tomorrow holds!

I left myself to itself, a self filled with the present.

Departure emptied me of temples.

Heaven has its own nations and wars.

I have a gazelle for a wife,

and palm trees for odes in a book of sand.

What I see is the past.

For mankind, a kingdom of dust and a crown.

Let my language overcome my hostile fate, my line of descendants.

Let it overcome me, my father, and a vanishing that won't vanish.

This is my language, my miracle, my magic wand.

This is my obelisk and the gardens of my Babylon,

my first identity, my polished metal, the desert idol of an Arab

who worships what flows from rhymes like stars in his *aba*,

and who worships his own words.

So let there be prose.

There must be a divine prose for the Prophet to triumph.

Night That Overflows My Body

This jasmine in the July night is a song
for two strangers who meet on a street leading nowhere.
Who am I after your two almond eyes? the male stranger asks.
Who am I after your exile in me? the female stranger asks.
Well, then, let us not stir the salt of ancient seas in a remembering body.
She was re-creating his warm flesh, and he, hers.
Thus the two loving strangers leave their love in disarray
the way they left their underwear among the flowery sheets.
—If you really were my beloved, then compose
a Song of Songs for me, and engrave my name
on the trunk of a pomegranate tree in the gardens of Babylon.
—If you truly love me, place my dream
in my hands, and say to the Son of Mary,
"Lord, how could you have made us endure what you endured yourself?
Will there be enough justice left over
for us to be just ourselves tomorrow?"
—How will jasmine heal me tomorrow?
—How will jasmine heal me tomorrow?
The shadows glow on the ceiling of their room, but they grow dim.
She tells him not to be gloomy after giving him her breast.
He says: *Your breast is a night illuminating*

what should be illuminated. A night that kisses me.

We were filled, the place and I, with a night that overflowed its cup.

She laughs at his description. Then laughs even harder

when she conceals the arch of the night in the palm of her hand.

—*O my beloved, if I were a boy, I would have been you.*

—*And if I were a girl, I would have been you.*

And she cries, as usual, when she returns from a sky the color of wine:

Stranger, take me to a country where I have no bluebird on a willow-branch.

And she cries to move through her forests

on the long journey toward herself:

Who am I? Who am I after your exile in my body?

Woe to me, woe to you, woe to my country.

—*Who am I after your two almond eyes?*

Show me my tomorrow!

Thus the two lovers bid farewell in disarray

like the smell of jasmine on July nights.

When July comes, jasmine carries me to a street leading nowhere.

But I still sing my song:

Jasmine on a night in July.

The Gypsy Woman Has a Tame Sky

You leave the wind sick in the mulberries.
As for me, I'll walk toward the sea so I can breathe.
Why did you do this to us? Why did you tire
of living in the quarter of the lily-of-the-valley, O gypsy?

We have all that you desire of gold and blood
recklessly passed down from dynasty to dynasty.
Stamp the icon of the universe with your heel
so that birds will alight on you.
There you'll find angels and a tame sky,
so do as you wish!
Crush hearts like a nutcracker.
Crush hearts and watch how the horse's blood spurts out!

Your hair belongs to no country. Your winds are homeless.
I'm without boundaries in the luminescence of your breasts.
From the laughing lilac of your night I pass alone down
the road of your fur, as if you created yourself.
O gypsy, what you have done with the clay of our flesh since last year?

You wear this place hastily as you would wear trousers of fire.
The earth's only task in your hands is to look back upon
the things of departure: water anklets, a wind guitar,

a flute to distance India even further.
Gypsy, don't leave us like an army leaving behind
its heart-breaking traces!

When you appeared to us in the sparrow's neighborhood,
we submissively opened our doors for all eternity.
Your tents are a guitar for vagabonds.
We get up and dance until the blood of the dusk settles
at your feet.
Your tents are a guitar for the old conqueror's horses
who attack to turn a place into myth.

Every time she hits a certain note, her jinn casts its spell on us.
And we are transported to another time.
We smash our pitchers one after another
so as to keep time with her rhythm.
We were neither good nor bad, just as in novels.
She was casting our fate with her ten fingers, note by note.

Will the cloud that doves bring back from sleep
return tomorrow? *No,* they say,
No, a gypsy girl never comes back.
She never crosses the same country twice.

Then who will mate the horses of this place with their own breed?
Who, after her, will polish the silver of this place?

from

A Bed for

the Stranger

1999

Translated by Sinan Antoon and edited by Munir Akash and Carolyn Forché

We Were without a Present

Let us go as we are: a free woman and loyal friend.
Let us go together on our separate paths.
Let us go as we are, separately and as one.
Nothing causes us pain—
not the final parting of the doves
nor the cold in our hands
nor the wind around the church.
All the blossoming almonds were not enough.
Smile, then, so that the almonds will bloom
even more between the butterflies of two dimples.

Soon we shall have another present.
If you look behind you, there is only exile:
your bedroom, the willows in the garden,
the river behind the buildings of glass,
and the café of our trysts.
All of them, all, are preparing to go into exile.
Let us be kind, then.

Let us go as we are: a free woman and a friend who is loyal to flutes.
We did not have time to grow old together,

to walk wearily to the cinema,

to witness the end of Athens' war with its neighbors

and the banquet of peace between Rome and Carthage.

Soon the birds will fly from one epoch to another.

A path of dust took the form of meaning

and led us on a brief journey between myths.

It was inevitable as we are inevitable.

Does the stranger see himself in the mirror

of another stranger?

—No, this is not the path to my body.

There is no "cultural solution" to existential concerns.

Wherever you are, there is heaven for me.

Who am I to give you back the Sun and Moon of the past?

Let us be kind . . .

Let us go as we are: a free lover and her poet.

All the snows of December were not enough.

Smile, then, so that the snow may be like cotton on

the prayers of the Christian.

In a while we'll return to our tomorrow, left behind,

there, where we were young and first in love,

like Romeo and Juliet learning the language of Shakespeare.

Butterflies fluttered out of sleep, as if they were

the spirits of a swift peace, giving us two stars,

but killing us in the struggle over a name

between two windows.

Let us go, then, and be kind.

Let us go as we are: a free woman and loyal friend.

Let us go as we are.

We arrived with the winds to Babylon and we march to Babylon . . .

My journey is not enough, that in my footsteps

the pines may utter praise for the southern place.

Here we are well.

Our wind is of the north, and our songs of the south.

Am I another you, and you, another I?

—This is not the path to the land of my freedom.

I will not be an "I" twice.

When yesterday has taken the place of my tomorrow,

and I have become two women,

I will be neither eastern nor western,

nor an olive giving shade to two Qur'anic verses.

Let us go, then.

There are no "collective solutions" for personal matters.

Being together was not enough for us to be together.

We were without a present to see where we were,

a free woman and an older friend.
Let us go together on our separate paths.
Let us go together
and let us be kind.

Sonnet II

Perhaps you ask only for ambiguity when you turn your back to the river.
There, an autumn sprinkles water onto a stag from a passing cloud.
There, on what you left behind of the crumbs of your departure.
The Milky Way is your ambiguity, the dust of nameless stars.
Your ambiguity is a night in pearls lighting nothing but water.
As for speech, it can light the night of someone setting forth
between two odes and two rows of palms, with the single word: *love*.

I am the one who saw his tomorrow when he saw you.
I am the one who saw gospels written by the last idolater,
on the slopes of Gilead before the old countries, and after.
I am the cloud returning to a fig tree which bears my name,
just as the sword bears the face of the slaughtered.
Perhaps when you turn your shadow to me, you bestow unto metaphor
the meaning of something that is about to happen.

The Stranger Finds Himself in the Stranger

We are two become one.

We have no name, strange woman,

when the stranger finds himself in the stranger.

What remains of the garden behind us is the power of the shadow.

Show what you will of your night's earth, and hide what you will.

We come hurriedly from the twilight of two places at once.

Together we searched for our addresses.

Follow your shadow, east of the *Song of Songs,*

herding sand grouse.

You will find a star residing in its own death.

Climb a deserted mountain,

you will find my yesterday coming full circle to my tomorrow.

You will find where we were and where, together, we will be.

We are two become one, strange man.

Go to the sea west of your book, and dive as lightly

as if you were riding two waves at birth,

you will find a thicket of seaweed and a green sky of water.

Dive as lightly as if you were nothing in nothing.

And you will find us together.

~

We are two become one.

We have yet to see how we were here, strange woman.

Two shadows opening and closing upon what had once been our two bodies.

A body appearing then disappearing in a body disappearing

in the confusion of unending duality.

We need to return to being two,

so we can go on embracing each other.

We have no name, strange woman,

when the stranger finds himself in the stranger!

The Land of the Stranger, the Serene Land

As with you, there is a land at the border of a land within me,
filled with you, or with your absence.
I do not know the songs you cry as I walk in your mist.
Let the land be what you gesture toward, and what you undertake.

Southerly, it never ceases to revolve around you and itself.
It has two brief stays in the sky: summer and winter.
As for spring and its moods, that is your affair alone.
Rise to any woman within you, and daisies will appear
on every window in the city, golden, like the summer of the *Little Prince*.
As for autumn, and interpreting it as tired gold, that is my affair.
When I feed the church's pigeons my bread, I forget the freedom of marble.
When you walk among statues, I follow the scent of mandarin.

Traveling around its images in your mirrors:
O my daughter, I have no mother, so give birth to me here.
Thus the land places its secret in the body,
and marries woman to man.
So take me to her, to you, to me.
There, here, within me and without.
And take me so that my soul will rest in you

and I can dwell in the serene land.

Heavenly, I have nothing to say about the land in you

except what the stranger says: *heavenly.*

Perhaps the strangers mispronounce Aramaic letters.

Perhaps they make their gods from the primitive materials

they find on riverbanks, but they do sing well.

This land is heavenly, like clouds lifting from jasmine.

Metaphorical, like the poem before it is written:

O son, I have no father, so give birth to me.

The land speaks to me when I pass gently over it.

In your crystal night glittering between butterflies,

there is no blood on the ploughs, and virginity renews itself.

There is no name for what life should be, except

what you did and what you do to my soul.

Inanna's Milk

Yours are the twins of prose and poetry,
as you fly from epoch to epoch,
safe and whole upon a cosmic *howdah* of stars—
your victims, your kind guards,
carry your seven skies caravan by caravan.

Those who tend your horses, approach the water
between your hands and the twin rivers:
The first among goddesses is the one most filled with us.
A loving Creator contemplates His works.
He is enchanted with them, and longs for them:
Shall I do again what I did before?
The sky's ink burns the scribes of your lightning.
Their descendents send swallows down upon
the Sumerian woman's procession, whether ascending or descending.

For you, stretched out in the corridor in silk shirt and gray trousers,
and not for metaphors of you that I awaken my wilderness and tell myself
that a moon will rise from my darkness.

Let the water rain down upon us from the Sumerian sky as it does in myths.
If my heart is sound, like the glass around us, fill it with your clouds

so that it may return to its people, dreamy and cloudy as a poor
    man's prayer.
And if it is wounded, do not stab it with a gazelle's horns,
for there are no longer any natural flowers near the Euphrates,
so that after the war my blood can return in the anemones.
And there is no jar in my temple for the goddesses' wine
in eternal Sumeria, in ephemeral Sumeria.

For you, slender one in the hall, with silky hands and a waist
for playfulness, not for symbols of you, I awaken my wilderness and say:
I will take this gazelle from its flock and gore myself with it!

I do not wish your bed to be song.
Let the Winged Bull of Iraq polish its horns with time,
and the temple split open in the silver of dawn.
Let death carry its metal instrument in the choir of old singers
for Nebuchadnezzar's sun.
But I, who come from another time, must have a horse befitting
    this wedding.
If there must be a moon, let it be high,
a high moon made in Baghdad, neither Arab, nor Persian,
nor claimed by the goddesses all around us.
Let it be free of memories and the wine of ancient kings.
Let us finish this sacred wedding, O daughter of the eternal moon.

Let us finish it here on the edge of the earth
in the place brought down by your hands
from the balcony of the vanishing paradise.

For you, reading the newspaper in the hallway, fighting the flu,
I say: *Take a cup of hot chamomile and two aspirin,*
so that Inanna's milk may settle in you
and we may know what time it is
at the meeting of the Two Rivers.

Who Am I, without Exile?

Stranger on the river bank,
like the river, water binds me to your name.
Nothing brings me back from this distance
to the oasis: neither war nor peace.
Nothing grants me entry into the gospels.
Nothing. Nothing shines from the shores
of ebb and flow between the Tigris and the Nile.
Nothing lifts me down from the Pharaoh's chariots.
Nothing carries me, or loads me with an idea:
neither nostalgia, nor promise.
What shall I do? What shall I do without exile
and a long night of gazing at the water?

Water binds me to your name.
Nothing takes me away from the butterflies of dream.
Nothing gives me reality: neither dust, nor fire.
What shall I do without the roses of Samarkand?
What shall I do in a square, where singers are
worn smooth by moonstones?

We have become weightless,
as light as our dwellings in distant winds.

We have, both of us, befriended the strange beings in the clouds.
We have both been freed from the gravity of the land of identity.
What shall we do?
What shall we do without exile
and long nights of gazing at the water?

Water binds me to your name.
Nothing is left of me except you.
Nothing is left of you except me—
a stranger caressing the thighs of a stranger.
O stranger, what will we do with what is left
of the stillness and the brief sleep between two myths?
Nothing carries us: neither path nor home.
Was this the same path from the beginning?
Or did our dreams find a Mongolian horse on a hill
and exchange us for him?
What shall we do?
What shall we do without exile?

Lesson from the Kama Sutra

Wait for her with an azure cup.

Wait for her in the evening at the spring, among perfumed roses.

Wait for her with the patience of a horse trained for mountains.

Wait for her with the distinctive, aesthetic taste of a prince.

Wait for her with seven pillows of cloud.

Wait for her with strands of womanly incense wafting.

Wait for her with the manly scent of sandalwood on horseback.

Wait for her and do not rush.

If she arrives late, wait for her.

If she arrives early, wait for her.

Do not frighten the birds in her braided hair.

Wait for her to sit in a garden at the peak of its flowering.

Wait for her so that she may breathe this air, so strange to her heart.

Wait for her to lift her garment from her leg, cloud by cloud.

And wait for her.

Take her to the balcony to watch the moon drowning in milk.

Wait for her and offer her water before wine.

Do not glance at the twin partridges sleeping on her chest.

Wait and gently touch her hand as she sets a cup on marble.

As if you are carrying the dew for her, wait.

Speak to her as a flute would to a frightened violin string, as if you knew what tomorrow would bring.

Wait, and polish the night for her ring by ring.

Wait for her until Night speaks to you thus:

There is no one alive but the two of you.

So take her gently to the death you so desire,

and wait.

Mural

2000

Translated by Munir Akash and Carolyn Forché

Mural

This is your name, she said
and vanished into the spiral corridor . . .

I see a heaven within reach. A white pigeon's wing lifts me toward
another childhood. I didn't dream that I had been
dreaming—everything is real.
Clearly, I laid myself to rest and flew.

I will be what I will be in the final celestial sphere.
Everything is white. The sea aboard a white cloud is white.
And white is the nothing in the white sky of the absolute.
I had been and I had been not.
Alone wandering through white eternity
arriving before my time.
Not a single angel appeared to ask me:
What have you done there in the earthly world?
I didn't hear the hymns of the blessed souls nor the sinners' moaning.
I am alone in that whiteness, I am alone.

At the gate of Judgment I feel no pain: neither time nor emotions.
I cannot sense the lightness of objects nor the weight of obsessions.
No one is there to ask: *Where is "my whereness" now?*

Where is the city of the dead? Where am I?
Here, in this no-where, in this no-time,
there is no nothingness and no being.

As if I have died before I know this vision,
I know that I am breaking through to the unknown,
that it is likely I am still alive somewhere
and know what I want.

One day, I will be what I want to be.
One day, I will be a thought that no sword
nor any book will bear to the wasteland.
A thought like rain on a mountain opened by a blade of grass.
There will be no victor, neither might nor justice, that fugitive!

One day, I will be what I want to be.
One day, I will be a bird, and will snatch my being out of my nothingness.

The more my wings burn, the more I near the truth and arise from the ashes.
I am the dreamer's speech, having forsaken body and soul
to continue my first journey to what set me on fire and vanished:
The Meaning. I am absence. The pursuit of heaven.

One day, I will be what I want to be.
One day, I will be a poet. Water will depend on my vision.
My language will be a metaphor for metaphor.

I don't speak. I don't allude to a place.

Place is my sin and my alibi.

I come from there.

My "here" leaps from my steps to my imagination.

I am what I was, and what I will be—created and destroyed by an ever
    expanding space.

One day, I will be what I want to be.

One day, I will be a grapevine.

After today, let summer press me.

Let passers-by drink my wine under the chandeliers of that sugary place.

I am the message and also the messenger,

the briefest of addresses and also the mail.

This is your name, she said

and vanished into a corridor of her whiteness.

This is your name. Learn it by heart and don't dispute with it.

Disdain tribal banners. Be a friend to your recumbent name.

Try it out on the dead and the living.

Practice its correct pronunciation with strangers.

Write it on the stone wall of a cave.

O my name, you will grow when I grow.

You will carry me and I will carry you.

Strangers are also brothers.

We'll enchant the woman with that weak letter dedicated to the flute.

O my name, where are we now? Tell me:

What is now and what is tomorrow?

What is time and what is space?

What is old and what is new?

One day, we'll be what we want to be.

The journey hadn't yet begun, the road hadn't ended.

The wise men had not yet reached their exile.

The exiled men hadn't yet attained their wisdom.

Of flowers, we only know anemones,

so let us then go to the highest mural.

Green and high is the land of my ode—the words of God at dawn.

And I am far away, far away.

In every wind a woman teases her poet.

—Give me my femininity and take

that shattered vastness you gave me as a gift.

There is nothing left for me,

save resting my eyes on the lake's wrinkled bosom.

~

Bear the burden of my future and grant me my past.

But leave us together.

After you, nothing departs and nothing returns.

—And take the ode if you wish. I have nothing in it but you.

Take your "I," I will complete my exile in your handwriting.

You can give it to the doves to mail.

Who among us is "I"? For "I" will be its end.

Between writing and speech a star will fall.

Memory swells our reflections.

We were born in the time of sword and flute, among fig and cactus.

Death was slower and more clear.

Death was a treaty among those near the mouth of the river.

But now, it works by itself at the press of a button.

The victim has no killer as witness

and the martyr doesn't recite his own testimony.

What wind brought you here?

Tell me the name of your wound,

and I will know the roads where we might twice become lost.

Every beat within you strikes me with pain, driving me back to a mythical time.

My own blood pains me, the salt as much as the vein.

~

In the shattered amphora, the women of the Syrian coast
moan on their endless trail and burn under the August sun.
Before I was born, I saw them on the footpath to the fountain.
I heard the water in their pottery mourning them:
gentler times come back when you return to the clouds.

The echo said: only the past of the mighty comes back climbing
the obelisks of that expanse.
Their relics are made of gold.
The least of them address tomorrow:
Give us this day our daily bread and make bearable our present time.
The transmigration of souls, incarnation, and eternity
are not for us.

The echo, utterly tired of my incurable hope
and of arguments about the nature of beauty, asks:
Who is next after Babylon?
Every time the road to heaven becomes clear,
every time the unknown discloses a certain end,
the song shatters, prayers decay and turn into prose.

The land of my ode is green and high, overlooking the basin of my abyss.
How strange is your significance.

Just being there, by yourself, you become a tribe.

I sang only to balance the rests between notes of the doves' mourning, not to
interpret what God says to Man.

I am not a prophet claiming revelation, or that my abyss reaches heaven.

By the full power of my language I am the stranger.

If I tame my feeling with the letter "Dhad," my feeling tames me with the
letter "Ya'."

Distant words dwell in an earth that revolves in the sphere of a higher star.

When words are so close, they are doomed to exile.

A book is not enough to say:

I find myself present in the fullness of absence.

Every time I seek my self I find others.

When I look for them, I see only my own strange self.

Am I an individual teeming with crowds?

I am the stranger. Tired of plodding across

the Milky Way to my beloved,

tired of my superficial qualities.

The word's form narrows. Its meaning expands.

I flood the banks of my word and look at myself in the mirror. *Am I he?*

Will I perform my role well in the last scene?

Had I already known the play or was it thrust upon me?

Is that me playing the role or did the victim change his testimony?

When the author digressed from the original text, to live in the post-modern,

and when the actor and audience disappeared from view.

At the door, I sat wondering: *Am I he?*

This is my language, this sound is the twinge of my blood.

Yet the author is not I.

If I come but don't arrive, this "I" isn't mine.

If I talk but don't speak, this "I" isn't mine.

The obscure letters reveal to me: *Write to be. Read to find.*

If you wish to speak, you must take action.

Thus your opposing pair becomes one in the meaning.

The transparent one within you is your ode.

Sailors surround me, but there is no harbor.

Vanity devoured my subtlest phrase and my most direct word.

I couldn't find the time to identify with my intermediate position.

I didn't ask yet about the blurring similarity between exit and entrance.

I couldn't find death so as to pursue life.

I found no voice to scream:

Time! You took me too far.

You deafened me to what the obscure letters reveal.

The real is the absolute unreal.

Time, who never waits for those delayed at birth,

keep our past newborn.

It's the only remembrance we have of you

when we were your friends, not the victims of your chariots.

Leave the past unchanged, unable to lead or be led.

I saw what the dead remember and what they forget.

Time spins through their watches but they don't age.

They never sense our death, nor perceive their life,

nothing of what I was or would be.

It's a chaos of personal pronouns.

"He" is in "I"—"he" is in "you." No more whole and no more part.

No living one to say to a dead man: *be me.*

Elements and feelings dissolve.

I can't see my body there.

I don't feel death's power, nor my first life,

as if I were another person.

Who am I? The dead or the newborn?

Time is zero. When death carried me into the haze

I was not thinking of birth,

for I was neither alive nor dead, where

there is no being or non-being.

~

You are better, said the nurse as she injected me with anesthetic:
Be calm and worthy of what you will dream in a short while.

I saw my French surgeon open my prison cell.
With the help of two policemen from the precinct, he beat me with a stick.

I saw my father returning from the pilgrimage,
faint from a *Hijazi* sunstroke,
pleading with a row of angels: *Douse my fire!*

I saw Moroccan youths playing soccer and throwing stones at me:
take your word and leave our mother, O father who missed the path to the
    graveyard.

I saw René Char sitting with Heidegger two meters from me.
I watched them drinking wine, and for them poetry didn't matter.
Their small talk was a beam of light and an unknown tomorrow
    awaited them.

I saw three of my friends crying, sewing my burial shroud with
    golden threads.

I saw al-Ma'arri chasing his critics away from his ode:
I am not blind to what you see.
Insight is light. It leads either to nothingness or madness.

~

I saw countries embracing me with the arms of morning.
Be worthy of the aroma of bread and summer flowers,
for your mother's clay oven is still lit, and the greeting is as warm as a loaf.

Green—the land of my ode is green.
A single river is enough for me to whisper to the butterfly: O *my sister.*
A single river is enough to tempt all ancient myths to ride falcons' wings
while falcons change flags on remote mountain peaks
where armies set up kingdoms of oblivion for me.
A nation is as great as its ode.
But weapons, for the dead and the living, enlarge the meaning of words.
Letters polish the sword hung in the belt of dawn,
and by means of songs, the desert expands or recedes.

I don't have enough time to tie my end to my beginning.

The shepherds took my story.
They went briskly into the green, and through the beauty of a ruin.
With trumpets and facile rhyme they overcame oblivion.
At the point of departure they left me with thorns of remembrance and
   never returned.

Our days are pastoral, meandering between the tribe and the city.
I couldn't find a special night for your *howdah* with its crowning mirage.

You said: *What's the use of my name without you?*

Call me, for I created you when you gave me my name,

and in possessing it, you killed me.

How did you kill me—me, the stranger of the night?

Allow me into your forests of desire, embrace me, hold me close.

Spread the pure bridal honey over the hive.

With the rage of all your storms scatter so as to recollect me.

Night is bestowing its spirit upon you, stranger, and all the stars witness that my
*   brothers will end my life with azure-blue water.*

So, having shattered my cup with my own hands, let the happy present
*   be mine.*

—Did you say anything that inspired a turning point for me?

—No. My life was there, outside me.

I am he who talks to himself:

My latest ode fell from a palm tree.

And, besieged by dualities, I am a life-long traveler to my interior.

But life deserves its obscurity and its sparrow.

I was not born to know that I will die, but to love the innermost of God's shadows.

Beauty leads me to the beautiful,

and I love your love unchained by its essence and attributes.

I am my own double.

~

I am he who talks to himself:

From the smallest things arise the greatest ideas.

Rhythm is not the creation of words,

but of two bodies become one in a long night.

I am he who talks to himself and tames memory—*are you me?*

The third one of us is fluttering between you and me:

Don't ever forget me, O death.

Lead us on our path to you, that we may know illumination.

For there is no sun and no moon lighting my body,

I left my shadow hanging on a boxthorn branch

and the place grew lighter. My wandering soul flew away with me.

I am he who talks to himself: *Young girl, what has desire done to you?*

The wind refines us and carries us like autumn's scent.

On my walking stick, my woman, you ripen and ripen.

Now, you can go on the "Road to Damascus," in no doubt of Revelation.

For the rest of our life we have only a guardian angel and two fluttering doves.

But the earth is a feast.

The earth is a feast for losers (and we are among them).

We are left in place as the echo of an epic hymn.

And like an old eagle's feathers, our tents are swept away with the wind.

We were kindhearted and self-denying even without the teachings of Jesus.

We weren't stronger than plants, except at the end of summer.
You are my reality. I am your question.
We inherited nothing but our names.
You are my garden, I am your shade,
in the final passage of an epic hymn.

We never share the goddesses' plans, those
who open their chanting with witchcraft and snares.
They used a mountain goat's horns to move
the place from its own time to another.

We would be better off if the stars in our sky weren't higher than
the stones of our well, and our prophets less insistent,
then soldiers wouldn't listen so closely to our eulogies.

Green is the land of my ode, green and fertile,
beloved by lyricists from generation to generation.
From my ode I received a Narcissus
gazing into his watery reflection,
the clear nuances of her synonyms,
and the precision of meaning.
I have received the likeness of the prophets' words from her on the roof of night.
I received a wise, forgotten mule on a hill from her,
making fun of both myth and reality.

From her I received the thick contradictions of the symbol.
Incarnation does not bring her back from remembrance,
and abstraction does not lift her into glorious illumination.

I received my other "I" from her,
writing its diary in the poet's notebook:
If this dream is not enough, then I should keep
an heroic vigil at the gate of exile.
From her I received the resonance
of my language between the walls.
It scrapes from the walls their sea salt
when a fierce heart betrays me.

My wisdom was higher than the Aghwar.
I told Satan: *No, do not inflict your tribulations upon me.*
Do not corner me into dualities.
Leave me as I am, uninterested in the Old Testament version.
Let me ascend to heaven, where my kingdom is.

Take our History, son of my father, take our History and freely do all you are
    inclined to do.

I have been given peace and tranquility.
The tiny wheat grain will nourish me
and my enemy brother.

My hour has not yet come.

Harvest-time has not yet come.

I have to enter the first sleep, put faith in my heart, then go to Cana of Galilee.

My hour has not yet come.

Perhaps something within me is tossing me away.

Perhaps I am another.

Fig groves, with their beautifully dressed girls, are not yet ripe.

The phoenix has not yet given birth to me.

No one is waiting there.

I came before time and also after time.

But there is no one to share what I see.

I am what I see. I am the distant one.

O self, who are you?

On the road, we are two. On Judgment Day we are one.

Take me to the mortal light to see my becoming in the other of me.

O self, what shall I be after you?

Where is my body—behind me or before you?

Who am I, O you? Create me as I created you.

Bless me with almond oil and wreathe my head with cedar.

Take me away from this valley to a white eternity.

Teach me your way of life, and as a particle in your sublime world, test me.

Help me to endure the boredom of immortality.

Be merciful when you cause roses to bloom from my blood.

~

Our moment has not yet come,

for there are no apostles who will measure

time with a bundle of late summer hay.

Does time come to an end?

Nor are there visiting angels to counsel our poets to abandon their past,

leaving it in twilight while shaping their tomorrow by hand.

O Anat, my special Goddess, sing.

Sing my first ode on Genesis anew.

May the narrators discover

the willow's birth in an autumn stone.

May the shepherds discover a well in the heart of song.

May life suddenly open on the wing of a butterfly fluttering over a rhyme

for those who do not care about meaning.

So sing, O Anat, my special Goddess.

I am the arrow and the prey. I am the elegist, the *muezzin* and the martyr.

I never said goodbye to the ruins.

Only once had I been what I was.

But it was enough to know how time

collapses like a Bedouin tent in the north wind,

how places rupture, how the past

becomes the ghost of a deserted temple.

Everything around me strikingly resembles me,

but I resemble nothing.

As if there were no room on earth

for those pitiful, sick lyricists, descendants of demons, who

when they dream their beautiful dreams,

breach all borders and teach love poetry to parrots.

I want to live . . . I have work to do aboard the ship.

Not the work of rescuing the bird from our hunger or seasickness

but to be eyewitness to the flood: what comes next?

What are the survivors to do with the old land?

Will they repeat the story?

What is the beginning? What is the end?

No one came back from the dead to tell us the truth.

Death, wait for me beyond this earth, in your kingdom.

Wait, while beside your tent I say a few words to what's left of my life.

I want to read all of Tarafah, so give me time.

The existentialists tempt me to exhaust every moment

with freedom, justice, and the wine of gods.

Death, give me time to arrange my funeral.

Give me time in this fleeting new spring.

I was born in spring to keep the orators from endlessly speaking

about this heartbreaking country, about the immortality

of fig and olive trees in the face of time and its armies.

~

I will say: Let me fall into the lap of the letter Nûn.
There my soul will be cleansed by Surat 'Al-Rahman.
Then walk with me in my ancestors' footsteps,
attuned to the flute's notes echoing through my timeless time.
Violet is the flower of frustration.
It reminds the dead of love's untimely death.
So don't lay violets on my grave.
Seven ears of wheat and a few red anemones
are enough if they are available.
If not, leave the church's roses to the church and to the newlyweds.

Death, wait while I pack my bag: a toothbrush, soap, a razor, cologne
    and clothes.
Is the weather mild there?
Does the weather in white eternity change?
Does it stay as it is in both autumn and winter?
Will one book be enough for me
to kill the no-time, or will I need a full library?
What language do they speak there,
common colloquial or classical Arabic?

Death, be an honest hunter who does not shoot a gazelle near the fountain.
Wait until I recover and regain the clarity of a mind in spring.

Let's be friendly, and frank.

My life is yours when it's been lived to the full.

In exchange, let me contemplate the stars.

No one has ever utterly died.

For souls, it is only a change of form and dwelling.

Death, O my shadow who leads me, O my third person,

emerald and olivine's irresolute color,

blood of a peacock, sniper of the wolf's heart,

sickness of imagination, have a seat.

Leave your hunting gear at the window and hang your heavy key chain on
the door.

Mighty one, don't gaze into my veins looking for some fatal flaw.

You are stronger than my breathing, stronger than medicine, and the strong
honey of bodily love.

You don't need some sickness in order to kill me.

So be nobler than the insects.

Be yourself—transparent, a clear message from the Unseen.

And like love, be a raging storm among trees.

Do not sit in the doorways like a beggar or a tax collector.

Do not become a traffic cop in the streets.

Be powerful, of well-tempered steel, and take off that fox mask.

Be gallant and knightly, and launch your mortal assaults.

Say whatever you wish to say:
I emerge from meaning to meaning.
Life is fluid, I distill it.
I introduce it to my domination and my measure.

Death, wait.
Have a seat and a glass of wine, but don't argue with me.
One such as you shouldn't argue with a mortal being.
As for me, I won't defy the servant of the Unseen.
Relax. Perhaps you are exhausted today,
dog-tired of warfare among the stars.
Who am I that you should pay me a visit?
Do you have the time to consider my poem?
Ah, no. It's none of your affair.
You are charged only with the earthly body of man,
not with his words and deeds.

O death, all the arts have defeated you, all the Mesopotamian songs.
The Egyptian obelisk, the Pharaoh's tombs, the engraved temple stones,
    all defeated you, all were victorious.
You cannot trap the immortal.
So do with us and with yourself whatever you wish.

I wish to live. I have work to do on this volcanic bit of geography.
Ever since the days of Lot, until the apocalypse of Hiroshima,

devastation has always been devastation.

I want to live here as if I am, forever,

burning with lust for the unknown.

Maybe "now" is much more distant. Maybe "yesterday" is nearer

and "tomorrow" already in the past.

But I grasp the hand of "now" that History may pass near me,

and not time that runs in circles, like the chaos of mountain goats.

Can I survive the speed of tomorrow's electronic time?

Can I survive the delay of my desert caravan?

I have work to do for the afterlife, as if tomorrow I will not be alive.

I have work to do for the eternal presence of today.

Hence I listen, little by little, to the ants in my heart:

Help me bear the brunt of my endurance.

I even listen to the gasping scream of the stone: *Free my body.*

In the violin, I see longing migrate from an earthly country to a

heavenly one.

I hold my dear one, eternity, in the palm of a woman's hand.

First, I was created. After a while, I fell in love.

Then I got bored to death.

Later on, in my grave, I opened my eyes

and saw the grasses mirroring me from time to time.

What use is Spring, then, if it does not bring joy to the dead,

and if it does not restore life and the bloom of oblivion after life?

That is one way to solve the riddle of poetry, the riddle of my tender poetry
    at least.
Dreams are our sole utterance.

Death, slip into obscurity, recline on the crystal of my days,
as one of my most lasting friends, an exile among beings.
You alone are the exile.
You have no life of your own.
Your life is nothing but my death.
You do not live, so neither do you die.
You abduct children when milk is thirsty for milk.
You were never an infant whose cradle was rocked by finches.
Horned stags and angels never had fun with you as they had with us,
    the butterflies' companions.
You alone are the exile, miserable one.
No woman to hold you to her breast.
No woman to share the passion with you of night stealing along
the language of desire, where earth and heaven merge within us.
You do not have a child who comes to you to say: *I love you, father.*
You alone are the exile. O king of kings, no praise for your scepter.
No falcons on your horse. No pearls in your crown. No banners, no holy trumpet.
How can you go about without guards or marching singers, like a cowardly thief?
That's you, your glorious majesty, monarch of death, the mighty, leader of a
    death-dealing Assyrian army.

So do with us and with yourself whatever you wish.

I wish to live and forget you.

I want to forget our life-long friendship

and to read only distant Heavens' decree.

Every time I ready myself for your coming,

you become more distant.

Each time I say: *Go away.*

Let me unite my two bodies into a body flowing with life.

Each time you appear between myself and I, mockingly you say:

Don't forget our appointment.—When is it?

—In the utmost forgetfulness, when all the world obediently

worships and puts faith in the wood of the temple

and the painting on the wall of the cave declaring:

These ruins are me and I am son to myself.

Where shall we meet?

Will you allow me to choose a café near the sea gate?

No. Do not go near the borders of God, O son of sin, son of Adam.

You were not born to question but to act.

Be a good friend, O Death.

Be a heady revelation and allow me to understand

the essence of your invisible wisdom.

Perhaps you were hasty when you taught Cain the art of shooting.

Perhaps you were slow in training the soul of Job to a lasting patience.

Maybe you saddled a horse, to kill me on my horse.

As if, when I remember forgetfulness,

my present time survives only in my language;

as if I am an everlasting present time, as if I should fly forever.

As if, since I've known you, my language has become addicted

to your cloud-white chariots, far above clouds of sleep,

higher than a feeling of complete freedom from all weather.

On the path of God, we are two blind Sufis possessed by a vision.

Go back, death! Go back safely!

Here, in this no-here and no-there, I am free.

Go back to your exile, alone.

Go back to your hunting tools, and wait for me near the sea.

Get the red wine ready for me to celebrate my return to the ailing earth.

Don't be rude and ruthless.

I won't come to sneer at you or to walk

on the water of the lake north of the soul.

Yet, being under your spell, I ignored the end of the poem.

I didn't escort my mother on my horse to marry my father.

I left the door open for a troubadour's Andalusia.

I chose to pause at the fence along the almonds and pomegranates,

to clean my ancestor's cloak of spider webs.

A foreign army was marching along the same roads,

measuring time with the same old war machine.

~

Death, is history your twin or your enemy, rising between two abysses?

A dove may nest and lay eggs in iron helmets.

Absinthe may sprout and grow in the wheels of a broken carriage.

So what effect will History, your twin or your enemy, have on nature

when holy rains are tossed earthward and earth becomes one with the heavens?

Death, wait for me at the sea gate, in the café of the romantics.

Your arrows missed their target this time, and I came back from the dead

only to bid farewell to what was veiled within me.

My soul is filled with wheat and I return to feed

the thrush alighting in my palm and upon my shoulders.

I came back to bid farewell to the land

that drinks my body and sows me as grass for the gazelle and the horse.

So wait for me while I finish my brief visit to space and time.

Thank you, life. Do not believe me if I return and I return not.

I was neither living nor dead.

Only you—you were alone, the utmost lonely one.

My nurse says: *You were raving in a fever.*
You were shouting: O heart, heart, take me to the restroom!

Of what use is the soul if my body is sick and no longer functions?
O heart, heart, bring my footsteps back!

I want to walk to the restroom on my own.

I forgot my arms, my legs, my knees, as well as gravity's apple.

I forgot the workings of my heart and Eve's garden at the beginning of forever.

I forgot the workings of my smallest organ, the use of my lungs.

I forgot how to speak, and am fearful for my language.

Leave everything else as it is, but bring my language back to life!

My nurse says: *You were delirious. You were crying out to me.*
I don't want to return to any one. I don't want to return to any country.
After this long absence, I want only to return to my language in the remotest
    depths of the dove's cooing.

My nurse says: *You were raving without end. You asked me:*
Is death what you are doing to me now, or is it the death of language?

Green is the land of my ode, green and high.

Slowly I write it down, slowly,

to the rhyme of seagulls in the book of water.

I bequeath to those who ask:

To whom shall we sing when salt poisons the dew?

Green it is. I write it the way the ears of wheat,

bent over by their own fullness, and mine,

are written in the book of the field.

Every time I befriend someone or become brother to the ear of wheat,

I learn how to survive both annihilation and its opposite:

I am the dying grain of wheat that grows green again.

In my death there is a certain life.

As if I am: as if I am not. No one died there on my behalf.

The dead learned nothing by heart except gratitude:

May God have mercy on us.

Remembering lost passages delights me:

I didn't give birth to a child to bear the burden of his father's death.

I prefer free marriage between words.

The female should find the right male

in poetry's drift toward prose.

My limbs will grow along a sycamore tree.

My heart will pour its earthly water upon one of the planets.

What might I be in death after my death?

What might I be in death before my death?

One who was without shape said: *Osiris was like you and me.*

The Son of Mary was like you and me.

But a wound at the right moment damages the ailing nothingness,

and moves beyond temporal death to become thought.

From what does the art of poetry arise?

From the heart's aptitude, from an inborn sense of the unknown,

from a red rose in a desert?
What is personal is not personal, what is cosmic is not cosmic.

As if I am. As if I am not.
Every time I listen to the heart the words of the Unseen flood me,
    and trees grow tall in me.
I fly from dream to dream but I am without end.
A few thousand poetic years ago, I was born in a darkness of white linen,
but I could not distinguish between the dream of myself and my self.

I am my dream, as if I am. As if I am not.
My language bids farewell to its pastoral accent
only after a flight to the North.
Our dogs grew quiet.
On the hillsides our goats vanished in fog
and a stray arrow pierced the face of certainty.
I'm tired of my galloping language—and reluctant to ask:
How does the past judge the days of Imru' al-Qays
who was torn between Caesar and poetry?

Every time I turn to face my gods, there is a land
of lavender and I bathe in the light of a moon ringed by Anat.
Anat is legend's guardian of metonymy.
She mourned no one except her excessive charm.

~

All this charm was for me alone?
Was there no poet to share the empty bed
of glory with me and to pick the many roses
at the fence of my womanhood?
Was there no poet who could coax the nightly milk from my bosom?
I am the beginning and the end. My limit exceeds my limit.
After me, gazelles will leap in my words.
O not before me . . . O not after me.

I will dream, but not to repair chariots of wind, nor to heal the wounded soul.

Myth has already taken its place—a plot within the real.

A poem cannot change a passing, yet still-present past,
    nor prevent an earthquake.

But I will dream. May a certain land take me in as I am, one of the sea
    of refugees.

Stop asking difficult questions about me, my place and whether my mother
    actually gave birth to me.

My mind is not woven of suspicions.

And I'm not under siege by shepherds and kings.

My present, like my future, is with me.

I also have my small notebook.

Every time a bird grazes a cloud I write it down.

The dream has untied my wings.

I, too, fly. Every living thing is a bird.
I am who I am, and no more.

I am of this plain. When the Feast of Barley comes, I visit my magnificent
    ruins.
They are tattooed on our identity. Winds don't blow them away
nor render them eternal, and in the Feast of the Vine,
I drink a glass of the wandering merchant's wine.
My soul is light. My body is heavily burdened with memories and with place.
In spring, I become a woman tourist's reflections written on a postcard:
On the left of the deserted stage, a lily and a strange man.
On the right, a modern city.

I am who I am, and nothing more.
I am not one of Rome's minions who guard the salt roads.
But I am forced to pay a percentage of the salt in my bread,
and I say to history: *Put slaves and kings in disguise on your trucks,*
and pass by. Now, no one says: No.

I am who I am, and nothing more.
One of the people of the night.
I dream I ride on horseback so high . . .
to find the fountain behind the hill.
So stand firm, O my horse!
In this wind, again, we are one.

You are my youth. I am your shadow.

Rise like an "I" and become lightning.

With our galloping of desire, pound the veins of an echo.

Ascend. Born anew. Rise upright like an "I."

Be tense, be rigid, my horse! Rise upright like an "I."

Don't stumble on this last slope like an abandoned letter of the alphabet.

In this wind, again, we are one. You are my alibi.

I am your metaphor, aloof from destiny's path.

O make haste, my horse, and stamp my time into my place.

The place is the path, but there is no path except you, who shoes the wind.

Make stars glitter in the mirage!

Let the clouds of absence sparkle with light!

Be my brother! Be the guide of my lightning, O my horse!

Don't die on this last slope before me, or after me, or with me.

Keep your eyes on the ambulance and on the dead, for it's possible I am still alive.

I will dream, not to correct any meaning beyond me,

but to heal the inner desolation of its terrible drought.

By heart, I learned all my heart.

My heart gave up curiosity and denied itself comfort.

My heart grew resigned and could be tamed with an aspirin.

It resembles my foreign neighbor, whose desires and woman I do not share.

~

Hearts rust like iron. They don't yearn or groan,
or become enraptured by the first raindrop of erotic passion.
They don't rattle from dryness like August grass.

My heart resembles a self-denying Sufi or an unwanted surplus of myself.
When the heart's water dries, aesthetics become more abstract,
passions wear cloaks, and virginity wraps itself in cleverness.

Every time I turn my face toward the early songs,
I see the trace of a partridge on the face in the words.
I didn't have a happy childhood, to allow me to say:
Yesterday was forever better.
But memory, with two light hands,
hungrily induces fever in the body of the earth.
Memory has the fragrance of a weeping night flower
arousing in the exile's blood a need for singing:
Lift up my grief, so I can retrieve my time.
I need one flap of a seagull's wings to follow the ancient ships.
How time has flown since we discovered those twins!
Time, and a natural death confused with life.

We still live as if death mistakes us. We—who are capable of remembrance
   —are capable of liberation.
We follow the green steps of Gilgamesh, time after time.

~

A complete being of nothingness . . .

Like a small jar of water, absence breaks in me.

Enkidu went to sleep and never woke up.

My wings also went to sleep, wrapped in a fistful of Enkidu's clay feathers.

My gods are a storm turned to stone in the land of the imagination.

My right arm is a wooden stick.

This heart is abandoned like a dry well,

as beastly echo expands:

Enkidu! My imagination is no longer enough for me to complete the journey.

I must have enough power to make my dream real.

Let me polish my weapons with the salt of tears.

Let there be tears, Enkidu, to help our dead mourn the living.

To which do I belong?

Who sleeps now, Enkidu? The man I am, or you?

My gods are grasping the wind.

So, with all your human recklessness, help me rise!

Dream of a humble balance between the heavenly and ourselves!

It's we who shape this beautiful land between the Tigris and the Euphrates,
    we who honor the names.

Have you tired of me, friend? Why did you abandon me?

Without our handsome youth what use is our wisdom?

At the mouth of the wilderness you left me alone.

Therefore, my friend, you murdered me.

I must foresee our fate alone, bitterly alone.

I must bear the weight of the earth on my shoulders

alone, and become an enraged bull.

I must search for my timelessness, lost and alone.

I must solve the riddle, Enkidu.

I will bear your life in place of you.

I will bear your burden to the end of my power and will.

Who am I, alone?

Overcome by a complete being of nothingness.

Yet I will rest your naked shadow against a palm tree.

But where is your shadow?

Where could it be after all your trunks have been destroyed? The apogee of
   man is an abyss.

In order to fight the beast in you, I asked a woman to give you milk.

I was unjust. But you were given pleasure, and you gave in.

Be kind to me, Enkidu. Go back to the dead.

It's possible we might find an answer

to the question of who we are when we are alone.

The life of a single man is not complete,

and I am in dire need of an answer to this question.

Whom can I ask about crossing this river?

So rise and lift me up, O brother in salt!

When you sleep, do you know you are sleeping?

Rise up! Enough.

Move before the wise men, like foxes, surround me.

All is vanity. Your life is a treasure, so live it, richly.

It's a single moment, promising its own sap—the distilled blood of
the prairie.

Live your waking, not your dream: Everything dies.

Live your life in a beloved woman.

Life is your body, not some illusion.

Wait for a child to carry in your soul.

For us, procreation is immortality.

And all is vanity and mortal, or mortal and vanity.

Who am I? The singer of the *Song of Songs?*

The wise one of Ecclesiastes? Or both?

A king, a poet and a wise man at the edge of the well,

I have no cloud in my hand.

There aren't eleven planets in the dome of my temple.

My body has become too small for me: so has eternity.

Like a crown of dust, my future is sitting there in my seat.

Vanity, vanity of vanities . . . vanity!

All that lives on earth is bound to pass.

Northern are the winds. Southern are the winds.

The sun rises from the sun. The sun sets into the sun.

The greatest absurdity is that nothing is new, and time is past.

The temples are high, and so are the ears of wheat.

When the sky descends there is rain.

When a country lifts itself up it withers.

Everything that exceeds its limit one day turns into its opposite.

Life on earth is the shadow of the unseen.

Vanity, vanity of vanities . . . vanity!

All that lives on earth is bound to pass.

1,400 chariots and 12,000 horses carry my golden name, generation to
     generation.

I lived as never a poet has. A king and a sage.

I grew old, tired of glory, all my wants satisfied.

Is this why the more I know, the louder I lament?

What use is Jerusalem?

What use is the throne to me?

Nothing abides forever.

A time to be born

and a time to die,

a time to speak

and a time to keep silent,

a time for war

and a time for peace.
All is bound to pass.
All rivers flow to the sea,
yet the sea is not filled.
Nothing abides forever.
All is bound to die,
yet death is not filled.
Nothing abides but my name in gold:
Once upon a time, Solomon . . .
What may the dead make of their names?
Does gold shine into my vast darkness
or *Ecclesiastes*
or the *Song of Songs?*

Vanity, vanity of vanities . . . vanity!
All that lives on earth is bound to pass.

As Christ walked on the lake, I walked in my vision.
Fearful of heights, I came down from the Cross,
and did not preach the Apocalypse.
I only changed my heartbeat to hear my heart more clearly.

Heroes have their eagles,
mine is a ring-necked dove,
a star lost over a roof,

a winding alley ending at the port of Acre,
no more, no less.
Where I left myself, a happy child,
I say to that self: *Good morning.*

(I wasn't a happy child at the time,
but distance is a skilled blacksmith
who can turn worthless iron into moonlight.)

—*Do you know me?* I asked a shadow near the rampart.
A girl dressed in flames saw me, and said: *Are you speaking to me?*
No, I said, *I was talking to a ghost that haunts me.*
Another Majnoon Laila roaming the ruins, she said,
then went into her shop at the end of the Old Souk.

Here we are—two palms loading the sea with some poets' letters.
We didn't age much, O self.
The sea-view, the wall that overlooks our defeat,
the heavy scent of incense, all bear witness:
we will still be here,
we are still here.
Perhaps we never took leave of each other.

—*Do you know me?*
Cried the young boy lost to me.

We didn't part, but we'll never be together again.

He tied two slippery waves to his arms and soared high.

Who is the immigrant? I asked.

At the western shore I asked the prison guard:

—*Are you the son of my old prison guard?*

—*Yes!*

—*Where is your father?*

He passed away years ago, he said.

The boredom of keeping watch exhausted him.

Then he bequeathed his daily work to me and begged me to save the city from
   your song.

I asked: *How long have you watched me and imprisoned yourself within me?*

He said: *Since you wrote your first songs.*

I said: *But you weren't born yet!*

He said: *I have time and I have eternity,*

I want to live like an American

but also within the walls of Jerusalem.

I said: *Be yourself. As for me, I have gone.*

The man you see is no longer myself!

I am my ghost.

He said: *Enough! Isn't your name the echo in the stones?*

Which is why you neither left nor returned.

You are still in this dull prison cell, so leave me alone.

~

I said: *Am I still here?*
Am I free, or still a prisoner without knowing it?
This sea beyond the wall is my sea.
He said: *You are a prisoner of yourself, a prisoner of longing.*
The man you see before you is not me. I am my ghost.

I told myself: *I am alive.*
And I said: *When two ghosts meet in the desert, do they walk on the*
   same sands?
Do they compete to overpower the night?

The port clock was still ticking all alone.
No one cared about the time of night.
The fishermen cast their nets, braiding the waves.
Lovers dance in the nightclub.
Dreamers stroke their sleeping nightingales and dream.
I said: *I will wake up when I die.*
I've had enough yesterdays; what I need is a tomorrow.
I'll follow my steps on the old path, the path of the sea air.
No woman will see me under her balcony.
There will be nothing left of memory except what I need in my endless travels.
In the old days, there were enough tomorrows.
I was lighter than butterflies, smaller than dimples.

Take my sleepiness and hide me in a story
in the tender evening under one or two palm trees.
Teach me poetry, that I may learn to wander Homer's lands.
May I add to the legend a portrait of Acre, the oldest of beautiful cities.
A stone box, both the living and the dead move
on this humming earth, like bees in their closed hive.
With every strong siege, they turn their faces into flowers
and ask the sea: *Which door leads to safety?*

Teach me poetry. A girl might need a song for her distant lover:
Take me to you, even by force. Hold my dream in the palm of your hand.
Embracing, they enter the echo, as if I had married off two lost gazelles.
I opened a church door to the doves . . . Teach me poetry.
This one, who spun the woolen shirt
and spent her time waiting at the door,
is more entitled to describe the enormity and the longing:
The warrior didn't return, or will not return.
I am not waiting for you.

Just as Christ walked on the lake, I walked in my vision.
Yet I came down from the Cross, fearing heights, and keeping silent about
    the Apocalypse.
I changed only my heartbeat to hear my heart more clearly.
Heroes have their eagles, mine is a ring-necked dove,
a star lost over a roof, an alley ending at the port.

This sea is mine. This fresh air is mine.

This sidewalk, my steps and my sperm on the sidewalk are mine.

The old bus station is mine.

Mine is the ghost and the haunted one.

The copper pots, *The Throne Verse,* and the key are mine.

The door, the guards and the bell are mine.

The horseshoe that flew over the walls is mine.

Mine is all that was mine.

The pages torn from the New Testament are mine.

The salt of my tears on the wall of my house is mine.

And my name, though I mispronounce it in five flat letters, is also mine.

This name is my friend's name, wherever he may be, and also mine.

Mine is the temporal body, present and absent.

Two meters of earth are enough for now.

A meter and seventy-five centimeters are enough for me.

The rest is for a chaos of brilliant flowers to slowly soak up my body.

What was mine: my yesterday.

What will be mine: the distant tomorrow,

and the return of the wandering soul as if nothing had happened.

And as if nothing had happened:

a slight cut in the arm of the absurd present.

History mocks its victims and its heroes.

It glances at them in passing and goes on.

The sea is mine. The fresh air is mine.

~

And my name, though I mispronounce it over the coffin, is mine.

As for me, filled with every reason to leave,

I am not mine.

I am not mine.

I am not mine.

Three Poems

before 1986

Translated by Munir Akash and Carolyn Forché

A Soldier Dreams of White Tulips

He dreams of white tulips, an olive branch, her breasts in evening blossom.
He dreams of a bird, he tells me, of lemon flowers.
He does not intellectualize about his dream. He understands things as he
    senses and smells them.
Homeland for him, he tells me, *is to drink my mother's coffee, to return*
    at nightfall.

And the land? *I don't know the land,* he said.
I don't feel it in my flesh and blood, as they say in the poems.
Suddenly I saw the land as one sees a grocery store, a street, newspapers.

I asked him, but don't you love the land? *My love is a picnic,* he said, *a glass of*
    wine, a love affair.
—*Would you die for the land?*
—*No!*
All my attachment to the land is no more than a story or a fiery speech!
They taught me to love it, but I never felt it in my heart.
I never knew its roots and branches, or the scent of its grass.

—*And what about its love? Did it burn like suns and desire?*
He looked straight at me and said: *I love it with my gun.*

And by unearthing feasts in the garbage of the past
and a deaf-mute idol whose age and meaning are unknown.

He told me about the moment of departure, how his mother
silently wept when they led him to the front,
how her anguished voice gave birth to a new hope in his flesh
that doves might flock through the Ministry of War.

He drew on his cigarette. He said, as if fleeing from a swamp of blood,
I dreamt of white tulips, an olive branch, a bird embracing the dawn on a
    lemon branch.
—*And what did you see?*
—*I saw what I did:*
a blood-red boxthorn.
I blasted them in the sand . . . in their chests . . . in their bellies.
—*How many did you kill?*
—*It's impossible to tell. I only got one medal.*

Pained, I asked him to tell me about one of the dead.

He shifted in his seat, fiddled with the folded newspaper,
then said, as if breaking into song:
He collapsed like a tent on stones, embracing shattered planets.
His high forehead was crowned with blood. His chest was empty of medals.

He was not a well-trained fighter, but seemed instead to be a peasant, a worker,
    or a peddler.
Like a tent he collapsed and died, his arms stretched out like dry creek-beds.
When I searched his pockets for a name, I found two photographs, one of his
    wife, the other of his daughter.

Did you feel sad? I asked.
Cutting me off, he said, *Mahmoud, my friend,*
sadness is a white bird that does not come near a battlefield.
Soldiers commit a sin when they feel sad.
I was there like a machine spitting hellfire and death,
turning space into a black bird.

He told me about his first love, and later, about distant streets,
about reactions to the war in the heroic radio and the press.
As he hid a cough in his handkerchief I asked him:
Shall we meet again?
Yes, but in a city far away.

When I filled his fourth glass, I asked jokingly:
Are you off? What about the homeland?
Give me a break, he replied.
I dream of white tulips, streets of song, a house of light.
I need a kind heart, not a bullet.

I need a bright day, not a mad, fascist moment of triumph.

I need a child to cherish a day of laughter, not a weapon of war.

I came to live for rising suns, not to witness their setting.

He said goodbye and went looking for white tulips,

a bird welcoming the dawn on an olive branch.

He understands things only as he senses and smells them.

Homeland for him, he said, *is to drink my mother's coffee, to return, safely,*

    at nightfall.

The End of Night (1967)

As Fate Would Have It

To Rashed Hussein

On Fifth Avenue he greeted me and burst into tears.
He leaned against a wall of glass
. . . New York is without willows.
He made me cry, and water returned to its rivers.
We had coffee, and too soon went separate ways.

For twenty years I have known him to be forty.
Tall and sad like the hymns of sea coasts.
He used to arrive like a sword dipped in wine,
and leave like the end of a prayer.
He used to read his poems at Christo's
when the city of Acre was just rising from sleep
and wading in the water.
It was a week for the homeland, a day for the invaders,
and a time for my mother to sigh.

There were roses and chains for his hands.
Nothing harmed him behind the fortress walls save the original wound.
Lovers come and toss their promises.

~

We rose over the thinning shores, beginning our feast of the vine.

We mingled in the breath of the wild rue.

We shattered all songs.

We were heart-broken by the black eyes of the assailant.

We fought and were killed, then we fought again.

Warriors come and go.

In every void, we see the singer's silence,

blue 'til the sun sets.

For twenty years he was tossing his flesh

to the four winds to feed the birds and fish.

It's time for my mother to sigh.

The son of peasants from the very rib of Palestine,

a southerner, wretched as a swallow.

Powerful with an airy voice and big feet.

The palm of his hand was beautiful. Poor as a butterfly and delicately brown.

Broad-shouldered, and could see beyond the prison gate.

He could see more sharply than a thesis on art:

he could see a cloud in a soldier's helmet.

He could see us, and also our food ration cards.

Plain-spoken and pleasant in cafés,

he liked flutes and beer.

His were the simplest words.
Easy, like water,
and simple, like a poor man's dinner.

He was a field of potatoes and corn.
He never liked school,
but he liked poetry and prose.
Perhaps the plains were his prose,
and the wheat his poetry.

He used to visit his family on Saturdays,
to take a rest from divine ink
and the questions of the police.
He only published two books of early poems
and left the rest to us.

Ten years ago he was seen walking through Lod Airport,
then he disappeared.

As fate would have it,
an ear of wheat gave me away,
then a sparrow led me to the killers' eyes.

As pale as the sun in New York:
Where could my heart pass the time?
Are there dove feathers in this stone jungle?

There's nothing in the mailbox,
and dawn here does not bite.
Even the brightest star is missing in the throng.

Evening is close. And my love's body is paper.
There is no one in my evening.
Wishing to be the river and the cloud.
Which way should the heart go?
Who will catch the dreams falling
near the Opera and the bank?
A storm of little pins batters
my most intimate pleasures.

I don't dream of anything now.
I desire only to desire.
I dream only of desiring harmony.

To desire, or to vanish.
No. It is not my time yet.

As pale as the sun in New York,
give me my arms, to embrace and my winds, to sail.

From café to café, in search of another language
to tell the difference between memory and hell,

searching for my original limbs.
I need my arms, to embrace and my winds, and sail.
Why does the ode abandon my heart
as soon as I leave Jaffa?
Every time I embrace Jaffa, she fades.
No. It is not my time yet.

He disappeared down Fifth Avenue—
the gate of the North Pole.
I only recall the cities in his eyes,
coming and going.
And he vanished, vanished.

A year later we met at Cairo Airport.
After thirty minutes he said:
I wish I were free
in the prison in Nazareth.

He slept for a week, and was awake for two days.
He didn't drift down the Nile to the countryside.
He drank only the color of his coffee.

In Egypt he could not see the Egyptian.
He only asked intellectuals
about the potential for class struggle.

Then the eternal question arose,

with its stony alienation.

I asked: *Who among the infidel prophets*

led you to so distance yourself?

He was saddened by my look of dismay.

Have you changed?

I have changed. My life was not in vain.

I depend on the Nile, he said. *The Nile is faithful.*

I said: *The Nile has a memory of steel, and is not*

as shallow as we thought.

And we retraced our past,

and the waves of swallows, above a hand beating against the wall,

the land that bred like insects in our veins.

And we remembered the rhythms of our past and the passing of our friends,

and those who shared our days,

then spread far and wide.

They didn't love us as we'd hoped they would.

They didn't love us, but they did acknowledge us.

He used to rave when he awoke,

and glisten when he cried.

He wandered around like a nomad's tent.

Life passed in vain.

I lost its essence.

~

He took in the sunset over the Nile . . . then vanished.
I arranged a funeral for him, of palm trees and a eulogy.

My endless suicide, put an end to my life.
So let's begin from any migration,
and, like the meadows of Galilee,
flood with light and burn like a victim.

My endless suicide, climb to the brow of the dream and fight.
The bells are ringing for you, and your clock
still strikes the hour.

He vanished.
The branches betrayed me.

As fate would have it,
the ear of wheat betrayed me.
A sparrow betrayed me to
the swords of the killers.

New York was inviting us into its official coffin.
On Fifth Avenue he greeted me and burst into tears.
He leaned against a stone fountain.
New York is without willows. He made me cry.
He restored the shade to its place.

Then we hid in the echo.
Have any one of us died? *No.*
Have you changed at all? *No.*
Is the journey still the journey
and the heart still a harbor? *Yes.*

He was far away, vanishing
into the endless unseen.
He drank his glass like smoke,
then vanished
as a gazelle vanishes in the disappearing meadows
beneath the fog.

He stubbed his cigarette out in my heart and rested.
He didn't look at his watch,
nor was he tempted by the trees
standing tall under our tenth-floor room in Manhattan.
He was wrapped in memories, and possessed
by the ringing of a mysterious bell.
Flocks of birds and familial deaths
flap at our hands and fly away.
This is not my time.
Another winter arrived.
Mares died grazing in the distant lands.

He said: *This is not my time.*
And I gave my heart for the collapse
of cities since life's origin perhaps,
until the end of the dream.
Do we stay in this orange day going outward
just to embrace the darkness within?

Where did you come from?
A bird struck an arrow.
So I said: *She discovered my heart.*
Do we stay in this orange day going inward
just to face the harbor police?

Freed of memory, he raves.
I carry the weight of the land,
and the savior from this waywardness.
Young women shoed my soul and were gone.
Birds nested in my voice, tore me apart, then flew away.
Nothing has changed.

The songs took my place, took my place.
This is not my time.
No. This is not my homeland.
No. This is not my body.

~

As fate would have it,
an ear of wheat betrayed him
then a sparrow lead him
to the winds of the killers.

Weddings (1975)

Four Personal Addresses

1. One square meter of prison.

It's the door, and beyond it is the paradise of the heart. Our things—and everything is ours—are interchangeable. And the door is a door, the door of metonymy, the door of legend. A door to keep September gentle. A door that invites fields to begin their wheat. The door has no door, yet I can go into my outside and love both what I see and what I do not see. All of these wonders and beauty are on earth—*there*—and yet the door has no door? My prison cell accepts no light except into myself. Peace be unto me. Peace be unto the sound barrier. I wrote ten poems to eulogize my freedom, here and there. I love the particles of sky that slip through the skylight—a meter of light where horses swim. And I love my mother's little things, the aroma of coffee in her dress when she opens the door of day to her flocks of hens. I love the fields between Autumn and Winter, the children of our prison guard, and the magazines displayed on a distant sidewalk. I also wrote twenty satiric poems about the place in which we have no place. My freedom is not to be as they want me to be, but to enlarge my prison cell, and carry on my song of the door. A door is a door, yet I can walk out within me, and so on and so forth.

2. *A seat on a train.*

Scarves that don't belong to us. Lovers at the last minute. The light of the station. Roses that deceive a heart in search of tenderness. Treacherous tears on the platform. Myths that don't belong to us. They traveled from *here.* Do we have a certain *there,* so that we might rejoice when we arrive? Tulips are not for us, so why should we love the railway? We travel in search of nothing, but we don't like trains when new stations are new places of exile. Lanterns, but not for us, to see our love waiting in the smoke. An express train to cross the lakes. In every pocket, keys to a house and a family photograph. All the passengers return to their families, but we do not return to any home.

We travel in search of nothing, so that we may achieve the rightness of butterflies. Windows, but not for us, to exchange greetings in every language. Was the earth any clearer when we rode the horses of the past? Where are these horses? Where are the maidens of the songs? And when in us are the songs of nature? I am distant even from my own distance. How distant, then, is Love? Fast girls, like robbers, hunt us. We forget addresses scrawled on train windows. We, who fall in love for ten minutes, cannot enter a house twice. We cannot become an echo twice.

3. An intensive care room.

When the earth presses against me, the wind spins me around. I have to fly, to bridle the wind, but I am a human being. In my heart, many flutes are tearing my breast. My sweat is like falling snow, so picture my grave in the palm of my hand. I was, little by little, tossed into bed, I threw up and lost consciousness for a while, and then I died. At the gate of that hurried death, I called out: *I love you, may I enter death in your feet?* And I died, I died utterly. How tranquil and peaceful is death without your crying? How tranquil and peaceful is death without your hands pounding on my chest to bring me back? Before and after death I loved you, and between I saw nothing but my mother's face.

It's the heart, set loose for a while, that has returned. I asked my beloved: *In which heart was I struck?* She leaned on my heart and answered with tears. O heart, how could you lie to me and let me tumble from my neighing horse? We still have considerable time, so hold out with me until a hoopoe from the Queen of Sheba's land comes to you.

We mailed letters. We crossed thirty seas and sixty coasts and yet we still have time to wander.

O heart, how could you fool a horse who loves the wind? Take your time until we finish this last embrace and fall to the earth in prayer.

Take your time that I may know whether you are my heart or her voice when she cried out: *Take me.*

4. A room in a hotel.

Peace be unto love when it comes, when it dies and changes lovers in hotels. Does it have anything to lose? We'll drink the evening coffee in the garden. We'll tell stories of exile in the night. Then we'll go to a room—two strangers searching for a night of compassion and so on and so forth.

We'll leave a few words on our two seats. We'll forget our cigarettes, so others may continue with the evening and the smoking. We'll forget some of our sleep on our pillows, so others may come and rest in our sleep and so on and so forth. How was it that we put faith in our bodies in those hotels? How could we depend on our secrets in those hotels? In the darkness that has joined our bodies, others may continue our cry and so on and so forth. We are only two of those who sleep in a public bed, a bed that belongs to all. We say only what transient lovers also said a while ago. Goodbye comes soon. Was this hasty encounter only so as to forget those who loved us in other hotels? Have you not said these wanton words to someone else? Have I not said these wanton words to someone else in another hotel, or have I said them in this very bed? We'll follow the same steps, so that others may come and follow the same steps and so on and so forth.

Glossary

Munir Akash

Aba   A loose, sleeveless robe woven of camel's or goat's hair. See *Webster's.*

Abu Firas, al-Hamdani (932–968)   Prince, knight, and poet of the Arab Hamdanid dynasty of Aleppo, Syria, whose members (like his cousin Saif Al-Dawlah, prince of Aleppo) were renowned as brilliant warriors and great patrons of Arabic poets and scholars. His most important concern was with the Byzantine Empire. He won a number of battles, but his worst defeat came in 962, when he was injured and captured by the Byzantine army. Spending many years in captivity, he wrote a series of poems known as the Byzantine Odes (*al-Rumiyyat*).

Al-Ma'arri, Abu Al-'Ala' (973–1057)   A great Arab poet, known for his virtuosity and for the originality and pessimism of his vision. He wrote many collections of poetry and the *Risalat Al-Ghufran* (English translation by G. Brackenbury, *Divine Comedy,* 1943), in which the poet visits Paradise and meets his predecessors, heathen poets who have found forgiveness. Al-Ma'arri, blind from childhood, called himself the doubly imprisoned captive in allusion to his voluntary confinement, and the loss of his sight. He suggested that children should not be conceived, in order to spare future generations the pains of life. In his will, he ordered the following verse to be written on his tombstone:

I owe this to the perpetration of my father
None owes the like perpetration to me.

Al-Mutanabbi, Ahmad ibn Husein (915–965) A poet regarded by many as the greatest in the Arabic language. He influenced Arabic poetry until the nineteenth century and has been widely quoted. He imparted a freer and more personal development to the traditional ode, writing in what might be called a neoclassical style.

Al-Rahman (the Merciful) One of God's ninety-nine names and one of the Qur'an's chapters (#55), in which the rhyme in most of the verses is in dual grammatical form and ends with the letter "N."

Al-Suhrawardi, Shihab al-Din (1155–1191) A mystic, theologian, and philosopher. He was a leading figure of the Illuminationist school of Islamic philosophy. His best-known work is *Hikmat al-ishraq (The Wisdom of Illumination).* He also founded a mystical order known as the *Ishraqiyah* (illuminationist).

Anat Ancient Canaan's most beloved deity, Anat was the moon goddess and the chief goddess of love and war, sister and helpmate of the god Baal. Considered a beautiful young girl, she was often designated "the Virgin" in ancient texts. Probably one of the best known of the Canaanite deities, she was famous for her youthful vigor and ferocity in battle. She was primarily known for her role in the myth of Baal's death and resurrection, in which she mourned and searched for him and finally helped to retrieve him from the netherworld.

Attar, Faridul-din (1142–1220) One of the greatest Muslim Sufi writers. Born in Iran and died in Mecca. His influential work *Manteq al-Tayr* (translated into English as *The Conference of the Birds*) is an allegorical poem describing the quest of the birds for the mythical Simorgh, or Phoenix. Other great works of this prolific poet include *Ilahi-nama (Book of God)* and *Mosibat-nama (Book of Affliction).*

Cana (Qana) The town of Galilee in Palestine where Jesus performed the miracle of transforming water into wine. Also the birthplace of Mahmoud Darwish.

Cordoba (English *Cordova*)   A city in southern Spain and the capital of Muslim Andalusia.

Dhad   An Arabic letter producing a very heavy *D* sound peculiar to Arabic. The Arabs are the people of *Dhad* or the children of *Dhad.*

Eleven Planets   The poet refers to the Qur'anic story of Joseph and his eleven brothers who betrayed him and desired his death. They took him away from his father and all agreed to throw him down to the bottom of the well (Qur'an 12:4–101).

Enkidu   See *Gilgamesh.*

Flute   See *Nay.*

Genghis Khan (1162–1227)   Mongol conqueror, born in Mongolia. His father's death made him ruler, at the age of thirteen, of most of the region between the Amur River and the Great Wall of China. In 1211 he began the conquest of Northern China and captured Peking, then swept westward, plundering Samarkand, Turkistan. He spread death and destruction through Persia, then across most of the Arab and Muslim world. The thirteenth-century chronicler Matthew Paris called Mongol a "detestable nation of Satan that poured out like devils from Tartarus so that they are rightly called Tartars." He was making a play on words with the classical word Tartarus (Hell) and the ancient tribal name of Tatar borne by some of the nomads. As the founder of the Mongol nation, the organizer of the Mongol armies, and the genius behind their campaigns, Genghis Khan must share the reputation of his people.

Gilgamesh (and *Enkidu*)   Gilgamesh ruled at Uruk in southern Mesopotamia sometime during the first half of the third millennium BCE. He was also mentioned in the Sumerian list of kings as reigning after the Flood.

He is the best known of all ancient Mesopotamian heroes. Numerous tales in the Akkadian language have been told about Gilgamesh, and the whole collection has been described as an odyssey—the odyssey of a king who did not want to die. The Ninevite version of the epic begins with a prologue in praise of Gilgamesh, part divine and part human, the great builder and warrior, knower of all things on land and sea. In order to curb Gilgamesh's seemingly harsh rule, the god Anu created Enkidu, a wild man who at first lived among animals. Soon, however, Enkidu was initiated into the ways of city life and traveled to Uruk, where Gilgamesh awaited him. Tablet II describes a trial of strength between the two men of which Gilgamesh was the victor; thereafter, Enkidu became friend and companion to Gilgamesh. In Tablets III–V, the two men set out together against Humbaba, the divinely appointed guardian of a remote cedar forest. In Tablet VI, Gilgamesh, who had returned to Uruk, rejected the marriage proposal of Ishtar, the goddess of love, and then, with Enkidu's aid, killed the divine bull that she had sent to destroy him. Tablet VII begins with Enkidu's account of a dream in which the gods Anu, Ea, and Shamash decide that he must die for slaying the bull. Enkidu fell ill and dreamed of the "house of dust" that awaited him. Gilgamesh's lament for his friend and the state funeral of Enkidu are narrated in Tablet VIII. Afterward, Gilgamesh made a dangerous journey (Tablets IX and X) in search of Utnapishtim, the survivor of the Babylonian Flood, in order to learn from him how to escape death. He finally reached Utnapishtim, who told him the story of the Flood and showed him where to find a plant that would renew youth (Tablet XI). But after Gilgamesh obtained the plant, it was seized by a serpent, and Gilgamesh unhappily returned to Uruk. An appendage to the epic, Tablet XII, related the loss of objects given to Gilgamesh by Ishtar. The epic ends with the return of the spirit of Enkidu, who promised to recover the objects and then gave a grim report on the underworld; see S. H. Hooke, *Middle Eastern Mythology* (New York: Penguin), 36–38, and the *Encyclopedia Britannica,* "Gilgamish."

Hijaz   The stretch from the Gulf of Aqaba on the Red Sea to a point about two hundred miles south of Mecca, Al-Hijaz, meaning "The Barrier."

Hoopoe (Upupa epops, Arabic *hudhud)*   Strikingly crested bird found from southern Europe and Africa to southeastern Asia. About eleven inches long, it is pinkish brown on the head and shoulders, with a long, black-tipped, erectile crest and black-and-white barred wings and tail. What is special about it is that, according to the Qur'an, the hoopoe was the bird that told Solomon about the Queen of Sheba and was the messenger between them; see the Qur'an 27:20–46. It is also the central Guide (*murshid*) in many Sufi works.

Howdah (Arabic *howdaj*)   A seat-covered pavillion on the back of a camel. See *Webster's*.

Hussein, Rashed (1936–1977)   A Palestinian poet in his own right, who paved the way for the rise of a new and innovative genre of Palestinian poetry later referred to as "The Poetry of Resistance." A pioneer who translated Bialik into Arabic and his native folktale into Hebrew. He lived a unique historical moment in the relation between Jews and Arabs, and is considered a bridge of mutual understanding by many Israelis. His life, which ended in a fire one winter night in a desolate New York apartment, is perhaps one of the most ironic tragedies in the annals of the Israeli occupation of Palestine; see *The World of Rashed Hussein,* ed. Kamal Boullata and Mirène Ghossien, Associaton of Arab-American University Graduates, 1979.

Hyksos   A group of mixed Semitic-Asiatics who settled in northern Egypt during the eighteenth century BC. In about 1630 they seized power, and Hyksos kings ruled Egypt as the fifteenth dynasty (c. 1630–1521 BC). See *Britannica.*

Ibn Sina, known in the West as Avicenna (980–1037)   A Muslim physician and the most famous and influential of the philosopher-scientists of Islam, he was particularly noted for his contributions in the fields of Aristotelian philosophy and medicine. He composed the *Kitab al-Shifa (Book of Healing),* a vast philosophical and scientific encyclopedia, and the *Qanun fi al-tibb (The Canon of Medicine),* an immense medical encyclopedia that became the textbook for medical education in medieval Europe.

Imru' al-Qays (died c. 550)   An Arab poet, acknowledged as the most distinguished poet of pre-Islamic times. He is author of one of the *Seven Odes* in the famed collection of pre-Islamic poetry *Al-Mu'allaqat*. Imru' al-Qays was the youngest son of Hijr, the last king of Kindah. He was twice expelled from his father's court for the erotic poetry he was fond of writing, and he assumed the life of a vagabond. After his father was murdered by a rebel Bedouin tribe, the Banu Asad, Imru' al-Qays was single-minded in his pursuit of revenge. He successfully attacked and routed the Banu Asad, but, unsatisfied, he went from tribe to tribe fruitlessly seeking further help. Through King al-Harith of Ghassan (northern Arabia), Imru' al-Qays was introduced to the Byzantine emperor Justinian I, who agreed to supply him with the troops needed to regain his kingdom. Darwish, in many of his poems, refers to this fatal journey and to the following lines of Imru' al-Qays:

> *My friend cried when he saw the road before him*
> *He realized that we were to seek Caesar.*
> *I said: do not shed a tear*
> *Either we try to gain the kingdom or die and are forgiven.*

Legend has it that upon his return to Arabia the emperor sent him a poisoned cloak, which caused his death at Ancyra (modern Ankara).

Inanna   The world's first goddess of recorded history and the beloved deity of the ancient Sumerians. In Sumerian mythology, she was known as "the Queen of Heaven and Earth" and was responsible for the growth of plants and animals and the fertility of humankind.

Inkishari (Turkish *Yeniçer*)   The Ottoman social rank of those born and raised to be professional soldiers. In 1622 they became extremely influential in the Ottoman court.

Ismael (English *Ishmael*)   A name.

Jaffa (Arabic *Yafa*)   A coastal Palestinian city (now in Israel).

Lisan al-Arab (*The Arab Tongue*)   An encyclopedic dictionary of the Arab language by Ibn Manzour (1232–1311).

Majnoon Laila   The story of Majnoon Laila is one of the most popular in the Arab and Muslim world, enduring in legends, tales, poems, songs, and epics from the Caucasus to Africa, and from the Atlantic to the Indian Ocean. Scholars find good reason to believe that the central character—Qays, nicknamed Majnoon (Madman)—lived in northern Arabia in the second half of the seventh century. Laila and Majnoon have been beloved figures for Sufi poets, as Krishna has been for the poets of India. The story, from beginning to end, is a lesson on the path of devotion, the experience of the soul in search of God.

Mu'allaqat   Collection of seven pre-Islamic Arabic odes, each considered to be its author's masterwork. Since the authors themselves are among the dozen or so most famous poets of the sixth century, the selection enjoys a unique position in Arabic literature.

Muezzin   The man who recites the call for prayers five times a day from the minaret of a mosque.

Naishapur   The birthplace of Omar Khayyam, a town in Khorasan, in northeast Iran.

Nay (English *flute*)   The *nay* is an extremely simple flute, composed of a reed with eight knots marking lengths of growth, pierced by seven holes. The mouthpiece is made of horn, ivory, or hard wood and has the shape of a truncated cone. It requires a very delicate technique, as only modifying the direction of breath can produce certain sounds. The position of the lips is such that a part of the air breathed out is refracted on the chamber of the mouthpiece, while the rest escapes, giving the *nay* a sonority very similar to that of human voices. This is why it is considered the sacred musical instrument of human passion.

Nebuchadnezzar   The name of three kings of Babylon. After the death of his father (604 BC), Nebuchadnezzar II reigned until 561 BC, conquering Syria and Palestine and, according to Jewish accounts, exiling 4,000 Jews. His restoration of Babylon made it one of the wonders of the world, famous for its hanging gardens.

Qalawoon, Sayf al-din (died 1290)   Sultan of Egypt (1279–90), founder of a dynasty that ruled the country for a century. Wishing both to expel the Crusaders from their remaining footholds in the Arab world and to repel the invading Mongols, he made a truce with the Knights Templars and then ended the Mongol threat to Egypt by defeating the Mongols at the Battle of Homs in 1281. In 1289 he broke his truce with the Crusaders and captured the fortified port of Tripoli, which was then the largest town still held by them. Qalawoon died while mounting a campaign to besiege the town of Acre. He was succeeded as sultan by his son Khalil, who successfully wrested Acre from the Crusaders in 1291.

Qat   Chewing *qat*—little green leaves—puts Yemenis into an afternoon haze. *Qat* is classified as a stimulant akin to amphetamines by the World Health Organization (WHO). But in Yemen, and throughout East African countries such as Somalia, Ethiopia, and Tanzania, *qat* chewing is an ingrained part of the culture that predates coffee drinking in other parts of the world.

Surah, Surat   A chapter of the Qur'an.

Tagore, Rabindranath (1861–1941)   An Indian poet and fictionist who was awarded the Nobel Prize for literature in 1913.

Tarafah, Ibn al-Abd   Arab poet, author of the longest of the *Seven Odes* in the celebrated collection of pre-Islamic poetry *al-Mu'allaqat.* Some critics judge him to be the greatest of the pre-Islamic poets, if not the greatest Arab poet. Some recent studies have highlighted his modern-sounding existential viewpoints and attitudes.

The Thorn Verse   This verse of the Qur'an (2:255) is very highly respected by Muslims. It's one of the verses that every Muslim learns by heart:
Allah! There is no God but Him / The Living, the Self-Sustaining,
Supporter of all / No slumber can seize him / Nor sleep. His are all things /
In the heavens and on earth / Who is there can intercede / In His presence

except / As He permitteth? He knoweth / What (appeareth to His creatures /
As) Before or After or Behind them / Nor shall they compass / Aught of His
knowledge / Except as He willeth / His Throne doth extend / Over the
heavens / And the Earth. And He feeleth / No fatigue in guarding / And
preserving them / For He is the Most High / The Supreme (in glory).

Thotmes   Egyptian pharaoh. As the key to so important a pass, the Palestinian town of Mageddo must have been fortified long before the invasion of Thotmes I, about 1600 BC. Thotmes III defeated the Syrian princes rallied there under the prince of Cades, after vigorous forced march, and on the following day they stormed the place, which he declared to be "worth a thousand cities." Traces of his assault are still visible on the ruins of the citadel.

Tiberias   Also called the Sea of Galilee, a lake in Palestine through which the Jordan River flows. The Sea of Galilee is especially well known to Christians because it was the scene of many episodes in the life of Christ.

Timur Lank / Tamerlane (1336–1405)   A descendant of Genghis Khan. In 1358 he won fame as a military leader, and by 1369 he became ruler of Samarkand. He conquered India, employing ninety elephants to carry back the treasures he had looted. He is chiefly remembered in the Arab mind and in history books for the barbarity of his conquests from India and Russia to the Mediterranean Sea, and for the cultural achievements of his dynasty. Timur Lank became master of the world from the Volga to the Ganges but no farther, for in his campaign against China he caught fever and died.

Designer:	Melissa Ehn
Compositor:	Wilsted & Taylor Publishing Services
Text:	Fairfield
Display:	Meta
Printer and binder:	Friesens Corporation